CAMPAIGN • 202

THE ARAB REVOLT 1916–18

Lawrence sets Arabia ablaze

DAVID MURPHY

ILLUSTRATED BY PETER DENNIS

Series editors Marcus Cowper and Nikolai Bogdanovic

First published in Great Britain in 2008 by Osprey Publishing,
Midland House, West Way, Botley, Oxford OX2 0PH, UK
44-02 23rd St, Suite 219, Long Island City, NY 11101, USA
Email: info@ospreypublishing.com

A CIP catalogue record for this book is available from the British Library

ISBN 978 1 84603 339 1

Editorial by Ilios Publishing Ltd, Oxford, UK (www.iliospublishing.com)
Page layout by The Black Spot
Index by Sandra Shotter
Typeset in Sabon and Myriad Pro
Maps by The Map Studio Ltd
3D bird's-eye views by The Black Spot
Battlescene illustrations by Peter Dennis
Originated by PDQ Digital Media Solutions
Printed in China through World Print Ltd.

12 13 14 15 16   12 11 10 9 8 7 6 5 4 3

www.ospreypublishing.com
Osprey Publishing is part of the Osprey Group.

DEDICATION

To my father, James Murphy, whose stories of travels in the Middle East first
inspired my interest in the Arab places. And to my sister, Sharon, for her
support and patience.

ACKNOWLEDGEMENTS

In the course of researching for this project many people have given
me help along the way. My special thanks go to Jean-Marie Linsolas and
Cyril Canet of the Service Historique de la Défense in Vincennes. I am also
grateful to Lieutenant-Colonel Rémy Porte of the Ecole Militaire in Paris.
The assistance of Louise Oliver of the Imperial War Museum in London
and Barbara Bair of the Library of Congress was also much appreciated.
I owe a very special debt of gratitude to Major Mesut Uyar of the Turkish
Army, whose expertise on the Ottoman Army was simply invaluable.
Neil Faulkner, John Winterburn and Angie Hibbit of the Great Arab Revolt
Project were especially helpful, providing advice and support and also
photographs of their excavations in Jordan. At Trinity College Dublin,
I would like to thank Dr W. E. Vaughan, Marcella Senior, Catherine Giltrap
and Brendan Dempsey. I also owe a huge debt of gratitude to Brian Patrick
Duggan for his help with this project. I would also like to thank Tommy
Graham of History Ireland and F. M. O'Connor of Wexford. My thanks go
to Marcus Cowper of Ilios Publishing for his help with this volume and
also Peter Dennis for turning a series of basic references into the excellent
artwork herein. Finally, I would like to thank Nathalie Genet-Rouffiac of the
SHD for the practical help, hospitality and the encouragement she gave
during the course of this project.

ARTIST'S NOTE

Readers may care to note that the original paintings from which the
colour plates in this book were prepared are available for private sale.
All reproduction copyright whatsoever is retained by the Publishers.
All enquiries should be addressed to:

Peter Dennis, Fieldhead, The Park, Mansfield, Notts, NG18 2AT, UK

The Publishers regret that they can enter into no correspondence upon
this matter.

IMPERIAL WAR MUSEUM COLLECTIONS

Some of the photos in this book come from the Imperial War Museum's
huge collections which cover all aspects of conflict involving Britain
and the Commonwealth since the start of the twentieth century.
These rich resources are available online to search, browse and buy at
www.iwmcollections.org.uk. In addition to Collections Online, you can
visit the Visitor Rooms where you can explore over 8 million photographs,
thousands of hours of moving images, the largest sound archive of its
kind in the world, thousands of diaries and letters written by people in
wartime, and a huge reference library. To make an appointment, call
(020) 7416 5320, or e-mail mail@iwm.org.uk.

Imperial War Museum www.iwm.org.uk

THE WOODLAND TRUST

Osprey Publishing are supporting the Woodland Trust, the UK's leading
woodland conservation charity, by funding the dedication of trees.

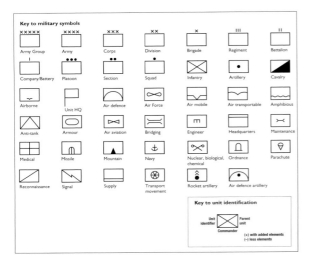

CONTENTS

Strategic situation in the Hejaz region of Arabia, 5 June 1916

At the outbreak of the Arab Revolt, the Hejaz region of Arabia was heavily garrisoned. Turkish forces were concentrated in garrisons in the coastal towns of the Red Sea while the crucial Hejaz Railway was garrisoned along its length. In the months preceding the revolt, Ottoman forces in the Hejaz had been reinforced with a significant build-up of troops at Medina, Ta'if and Mecca.

On the morning of 5 June 1916 the main garrisons at Medina and Mecca were attacked by tribal forces in an attempt to seize the main centres of Ottoman power in the region.

SINAI

Aqaba

Mudawwarah

Wadi Sirhan

THE GREAT NEFUDH

AL-HOUL

Hejaz Railway

ARABIA

129 (-) El Kurr

129 (-) Wejh

RED SEA

Um Lejj

Aba el Na'am

FAKHRI PASHA

Medina

ALI + FEISAL

129 (-) Nakhl Mubarak

45 Yanbu

Hamra

Bir ash-Sheikh

Masturah

Rabegh

EGYPT

Jiddah

Mecca

GALIB PASHA
Ta'if

22

HUSSEIN

Wadi

Turks

Arabs/British

N

0   50 miles

0   100km

ORIGINS OF THE CAMPAIGN

The Arabian subcontinent covers a vast area. It would be possible to fit all of the countries of Western Europe into it and still have plenty of space left over. At the outbreak of World War I in 1914, the majority of Arabia formed part of the Ottoman Empire. The exceptions were the territories included in the British protectorates of Kuwait, Aden and the Hadramawt and Oman coastlines. Today, the Ottoman territories would encompass the modern Arab states of Jordan, Yemen and Saudi Arabia. To the north and the north-east, the Arabian region of the Ottoman Empire was bordered by Palestine, Lebanon, Syria and Mesopotamia (Iraq), which were also part of the empire.

Ottoman power, therefore, stretched from Constantinople (Istanbul) in European Turkey as far as Hudayda in the Yemen. Its citizens included Muslims of both Sunni and Shi'ite traditions, Christians of various traditions and also Jews. While Ottoman rule in Arabia had been consolidated in the 16th century, by 1914 the relationship with the tribal peoples of this region of the empire was in many cases far from cordial. The total population of Arabia and the territories stretching as far as Syria numbered around six million people and this included both settled and nomadic Arabs.

Arab tribesmen on the march, 1917. Inured to life in the desert, they made excellent guerrilla fighters. In 1916, few suspected them of being capable of mounting a two-year campaign against Ottoman forces. (IWM Q58939)

The years immediately preceding the outbreak of the war saw the development of a growing discontent among the population of these regions. The wider population within the Ottoman Empire recognized that the administration had changed following the 'Young Turk' revolution of 1908/09, which had dethroned Sultan Abdülhamit II. While Ottoman sultans continued to rule for another 14 years, actual power was now in the hands of the members of the Committee of Union and Progress. In real terms, political control was exercised by Talat Pasha (Minister of the Interior), Enver Pasha (Minister of War) and Mehmed Cemal Pasha ('Büyük' or Djemal Pasha, Minister of the Marine). Relations between the Arab leaders and this new regime were initially cordial, they soon soured as the more tolerant Ottoman approach to the administration of the regions was replaced by a more authoritarian form of government. For many, it became obvious that the Ottoman Islamic Empire had been replaced by a Turkish Empire.

This growing discontent was also set against a backdrop of real military difficulty for the Turkish Government. During the 19th century, the Ottoman Empire had lost control of large areas of its territory following a series of military defeats. Egypt, which had formerly been an Ottoman province, was now effectively in British control. The years that immediately followed the founding of the Young Turk government had seen a series of international confrontations. In 1908, Turkey lost Bosnia-Herzegovina to Austria-Hungary. Following a campaign in North Africa in 1911/12, it lost Libya to Italy and, after the First Balkan War of 1912, it lost control of Macedonia. Before the outbreak of World War I therefore, it seemed that the Ottoman or Turkish Empire was on the brink of collapse, an event that had been predicted by many since the mid-19th century.

From an international perspective, the apparent political and military weakness of the Ottoman Empire was doubly worrying as it came at a time of increasing German influence within Turkey. Britain and France found that their links with Turkey, which had once been strong, were being constantly eroded while at the same time Germany was openly wooing the new administration.

Kaiser Wilhelm II visited Turkey in 1889 and 1898 and these visits coincided with a phase of German interest and investment in the Ottoman Empire. This soon came to be focused on railway projects as Germany supplied the engineers, railway equipment and funding for a series of railways across the Ottoman Empire. The most controversial of these was the Constantinople–Baghdad Railway, which was begun in 1888 but became the subject of international protests from Britain. In 1892, a new rail link was built to link Constantinople with Ankara. From an Arab perspective, the Hejaz Railway, which was completed between 1900 and 1908 not only facilitated pilgrimages to the holy cities of Mecca and Medina but also consolidated Ottoman power in the Hejaz. The German influence in all of these projects was worrying and in the years immediately before World War I, this influence began to focus on overtly military issues. There had been a German military mission in Turkey between 1886 and 1895 and, in December 1913, a new mission was established under the command of General Liman von Sanders. This German mission then facilitated the re-arming and reform of the Ottoman Army, providing instructors for new weaponry and also allowing Ottoman officers to attend German military colleges.

Against this backdrop of international tension, among the peoples of Syria, Mesopotamia, Palestine and Arabia the forces of nationalism were also at work. This was reflected in the development of a number of secret societies.

In Mesopotamia the Ahad society was formed, which included many Ottoman army officers of Iraqi birth. The most prominent society in Syria was the al-Fatat society, which was predominantly urban based and included intellectuals, civil servants and men of the landed class in its numbers. The overlord of Syria, Nuri ash Shalaan, contemplated revolt but was too near the seat of Turkish power to be able to do so effectively. There was a series of crackdowns on these secret societies between 1914 and 1916, which saw several of the leaders executed.

Further south in Arabia, there was also much discontent among the tribal peoples and this focused on the perceived irreligious nature of the new Turkish Government and, in more practical terms, its taxation policies. Abdul Aziz ibn Saud, who was affiliated with the fanatical Wahabi sect, controlled central Arabia with his centre of power at Najd. In 1914, however, he was isolated and far from sources of possible military aid. It must also be pointed out that several tribes remained fiercely loyal to the Ottoman Government. The most significant of these was the Shammar tribe, led by Ibn Rashid, which dominated north-central Arabia and had its power base at Ha'il.

Sharif Hussein ibn Ali photographed in December 1916. The Arab leader in the holy city of Mecca, it was he and his sons who instigated the revolt against Ottoman rule in June 1916. (IWM Q59888)

Increasingly, the focus of the potential revolt came to the centre of the Hejaz region of Arabia, which bordered the Red Sea and also included the holy cities of both Mecca and Medina. The Hashemite clan, direct descendants of the Prophet Muhammad who traditionally controlled the holy cities, ruled this region. The head of the clan, Sharif Hussein ibn Ali, became the focus of nationalist aspirations in the region. Before the war had even broken out, he had sent his second son, the Emir Abdullah ibn Hussein, on a secret mission to Cairo. While there, Abdullah met with Lord Kitchener, who was then commander-in-chief in Egypt. Kitchener, who had much experience of Egypt and the wider Red Sea area, recognized the potential of a revolt in Arabia against the Ottoman Government and gave the scheme his tacit approval. His appointment as Minister of War in August 1914 effectively removed him from the Middle East theatre of operations and perhaps denied the Arabs one of their greatest potential allies. Nevertheless, after Britain's formal declaration of war against Turkey in November 1914, Arab revolutionary plans acquired a greater significance in British strategy. Throughout 1915 links were maintained with the Red Sea port towns of the Hejaz and both small arms and money were shipped to Arabia in aid of the Hashemite cause.

Despite the fact that Britain had been sending military aid to the Hejaz throughout 1915, the outbreak of the revolt took the British staff in Cairo, and the world in general, by surprise. In the summer of 1916, the immediate revolt of Hashemite Arabs against Ottoman rule seemed unlikely. The fortunes of the main Allied powers were at a low ebb. On the Western Front not only were both the main Allied armies bogged down but France was still enduring the continued German offensive at Verdun. Previous Allied efforts against the Ottomans had also not fared well. The Gallipoli operation had come to an inglorious end in January 1916 while Britain's campaign in Mesopotamia was producing further humiliations, General Townshend having surrendered at Kut on 30 April. Throughout 1915 and 1916, Britain seemed paralysed along the Suez Canal and also in Aden.

A series of short-term factors forced Sharif Hussein's hand. It now seems certain that he was being pressured by Arab nationalists both from within his own camp and from as far away as Syria to take immediate action. Religious factors also played a part as Islamic leaders urged a holy war, or jihad, against the Ottomans who had entered into an alliance with Germany and Austria-Hungary, both infidel nations. Hussein would also seem to have feared a crackdown against those who opposed the Ottoman administration in the Hejaz. Given the recent execution of nationalist leaders in Damascus, he was probably in no doubt about what his own fate would be, and also that of his sons. His contacts in Constantinople informed him that Sharif Ali Haidar, leader of the rival Zaid branch of the Prophet Muhammad's descendents, was being groomed by the Ottoman Government to replace him as emir of Mecca. For their part, the Ottoman command was not insensible to developments in the Hejaz and, since May 1916, had begun moving increasing numbers of troops to the region. For Hussein and the Hashemite cause, quick action became imperative and, on 10 June 1916, the flag of revolt was raised at Mecca.

As the revolt was breaking out, T. E. Lawrence was a lowly lieutenant working for the Intelligence Department in Cairo. Regardless of his own sense of self-belief, it is certain that he never imagined that the events of the next two years would place him in the public eye to such a degree as they did. By 1920, he would be enjoying an international reputation, but in 1916 there seemed to be no potential for this situation to come about.

CHRONOLOGY

1914

April The Emir Abdullah ibn Hussein, the son of Sharif Hussein of Mecca, travels to Cairo for secret negotiations with Lord Kitchener and the British military and political staff.

29 October The Ottoman Empire declares war on the Allied powers.

1915 Arms and money are shipped by the British across the Red Sea to the forces of Sharif Hussein of Mecca throughout the year, in the hope of encouraging a revolt against Ottoman rule. Early in the year, the Arab forces make contact with the revolutionary al-Fatat organization in Damascus.

1916

January–July General Sir Archibald Murray leads his army in a gradual advance through Sinai.

February Representatives of the British and French governments (Sir Mark Sykes and M. Georges Picot) formulate an agreement for the division of Turkish territory following the defeat of the Ottoman Empire. This comes to be known as the 'Sykes–Picot Agreement'. It envisages British control of Mesopotamia (Iraq), Palestine and Transjordan (Jordan) whilst France was to control Syria, Lebanon and Turkish Cilicia. Russia was to receive the Armenian and Kurdish territories to the north-east of Ottoman territory.

May The Ottoman Government tries to block the importation of military supplies into the Hejaz region of Arabia. An Ottoman army in Damascus is prepared to travel to Arabia in the event of rebellion.

The Allied powers ratify the secret Sykes–Picot Agreement.

5 June The emirs Ali and Feisal announce the Arabs' intention to withdraw from the Ottoman Empire to the Turkish commander at Medina, General Fakhri Pasha. After attacks on the railway and a failed assault on the town, the Arab forces are driven off.

10 June Sharif Hussein of Mecca proclaims the revolt at Mecca; the Emir Abdullah attacks the Turkish garrison at Ta'if. Both towns finally fall into Arab hands some weeks later on the arrival of Egyptian artillery.

16 June The port of Jiddah is also captured, the Arab tribesmen being supported by the Royal Navy seaplane carrier HMS *Ben-My-Chree*.

30 June British military officers land at Jiddah, bringing mountain guns, machine guns, small arms and 1.2 million rounds of ammunition. They also bring food, money and a party of artillerymen from the Egyptian Army.

July The port towns of Rabegh and Yanbu are captured by Arab forces.

9 July	Last of Turkish garrison surrenders at Mecca.
1 September	The first members of the French Military Mission arrive in Alexandria in Egypt and soon afterwards are shipped to Arabia.
	Hussein takes the title 'king of the Arabs'. The British political staff later encourages him to change this to 'king of the Hejaz'.
22 September	Last of the Turkish garrison surrenders at Ta'if.
October	A British liaison party arrives at Jiddah. This party includes Lieutenant T. E. Lawrence.
November	Colonel Joyce moves to Rabegh, bringing weapons, supplies and a contingent of 450 Egyptian troops. He prepares to defend the town against a Turkish counterattack.
December	Lawrence is appointed as official adviser to the Emir Feisal.
	A Turkish counteroffensive threatens both Rabegh and Yanbu but draws off because of Arab resistance and also logistical difficulties.

1917

8–9 January	Battle of Magruntein: Turkish troops defeated in Sinai by British forces.
17 January	Fakhri Pasha calls off counteroffensive against Rabegh and Yanbu.
23–24 January	The Red Sea port of Wejh is captured by Arab forces, supported by an RN landing party.
February	Lieutenant H. Garland becomes the first Allied officer to mine a moving locomotive on the Hejaz Railway. At the same time, Capitaine Raho of the French mission undertakes a raid on the railway with a small party of Bedouin.

26 March	British defeated at First Battle of Gaza. On the same day, Lawrence leaves on a railway raid. This force of just under 400 men attacks the station at Aba el Na'am, north of Medina, on 30 March. Using a Krupp mountain gun, the station and some rolling stock are damaged. A mine destroys a locomotive and around 30 Turkish troops are taken prisoner. The line is cut for three days. Heavy fighting between Turkish forces and the Arab Southern Army near Medina.
17–19 April	Second Battle of Gaza. British attack unsuccessful. Murray replaced by General Sir Edmund Allenby.
6 July	After a two-month march through the desert, Lawrence and a force of Arab tribesmen to capture Aqaba. This strategic port is then used as the main base of the Arab Northern Army in its later campaigns in Palestine and Syria.
6–16 July	Colonel Joyce, Colonel Newcombe and a party of Sharifian regulars embark on a series of highly successful railway raids to the north and south of al 'Ula and also on Sahl al Matran. On 6 July alone, they detonate over 500 charges on the line.
24–30 August	Capitaine Raho and a party of 40 French troops and 200 Bedouin carry out a raid on the railway line to the north of Mudurij, destroying five kilometres of track and four bridges.
26 September to 1 October	Lawrence and Capitaine Pisani of the French mission embark on a railway raid with a party of around 80 Bedouin. On 6 October they destroy a train and a bridge near Akabat el Hajazia.
12 October	Colonel Joyce and a detachment of Sharifian regulars set off on a raid from Aqaba. They capture the ancient Crusader castle at Shawbak, which commands the road northwards into Palestine.

21 October	A large Turkish force is repelled by soldiers of the Arab Regular Army at Wadi Musa, near Petra.
31 October	Third Battle of Gaza. The British Army turns the Turkish flank at Beersheba. Lawrence leads a diversionary raid into Syria in an unsuccessful attempt to wreck the vital railway bridge over the Yarmuk at Tell ash-Shehab. With a party of Arab tribesmen and Indian soldiers, Lawrence leads an abortive attack on this bridge during the night of 7/8 November.
October to December	Turkish forces in Medina engage in a series of sweeps to the west to drive Arab forces away from the town.
2 November	In a letter to Lord Rothschild, the British foreign secretary, Lord Balfour, announces his support for the establishment of a Jewish homeland in Palestine. This comes to be known as the 'Balfour Declaration'.
November	A train is ambushed north of al 'Ula and is found to be carrying a large quantity of gold and a conciliatory letter from the Ottoman Government to Sharif Hussein.
20 November	Lawrence is captured, tortured and raped at Deraa.
9 December	General Allenby enters Jerusalem at the head of an Allied army. Lawrence is present at the official parade.
December	Colonel Joyce tries to explain the Sykes–Picot Agreement to Sharif Hussein in a positive light.
26 December	Lawrence and Joyce embark on a long-range reconnaissance towards the railway station at Mudawwarah, using Rolls-Royce armoured cars.

1918

1 January	Lawrence and Joyce use light artillery mounted on Talbot cars to attack Turkish posts north of Mudawwarah.
3 January	A force of over 1,000 Arab tribesmen and regulars led by Sharif Nasir and Nuri as-Sa'id capture the strategic well at Abu al-Lissan. They then embark on a large raid towards Ma'an and attack the station at Jurf ad Darawish on their return.
25 January	With a party of around 600 tribesmen, Lawrence defeats a Turkish column of 1,000 men at Tafila, a town to the south-east of the Dead Sea. The Arab force captured over 200 prisoners and also mountain guns in what was the most significant Arab victory over conventional troops in the war. Lawrence was later awarded a DSO for his part in this action.
March	Lieutenant-Colonel Alan Dawney replaces Joyce as head of Operation *Hedgehog*, owing to the latter being ill with pneumonia.
26–31 March	General Allenby leads an attack against Amman.
12 April	Nuri as-Sa'id, a former Ottoman officer now in Sharifian service, captures Ghadir el Haj using a party of the Arab regular army and a battery of 65mm guns supplied by the French.
13 April	Maulud Bey occupies Jabal Simnah, to the west of Ma'an using regular Sharifian troops. Further assaults on Ma'an during the days that follow.
17 April	A contingent of the Arab Regular Army and also Arab tribesmen begin a final major assault on Ma'an. The town does not fall but the railway line south of Ma'an is cut and is not repaired for the remainder of the war. A lengthy siege then ensues.
30 April to 3 May	General Allenby leads a second attack on Amman.
May	A series of raids takes place against the Hejaz Railway and 25 bridges are destroyed. This is part of a wider

campaign in support of General Allenby's operations.

4 June
The Emir Feisal and Chaim Weizmann, the Zionist leader, meet at Waheida to discuss the future of Palestine and also Arab claims to nationhood. Colonel Joyce acts as interpreter and later reports that both men were non-committal but positive.

8 August
A force of over 300 men of the Imperial Camel Corps commanded by Major Buxton and T. E. Lawrence attack and capture the railway station at Mudawwarah. RAF planes assist them in this.

16 September to 1 October
The Arab Northern Army under Feisal begins a new campaign in cooperation with Allenby's planned Megiddo offensive. A contingent of around 1,000 men including 450 Arab regulars, Gurkhas, Egyptian troops and French artillery carry out a series of raids on the line to the north and south of Deraa.

19 September
Allenby's Megiddo offensive begins. Arab attacks in and around Deraa continue to thwart Turkish attempts to repair the line. Despite being harassed by bombing raids from German and Turkish aircraft, the Arab Army continues to destroy bridges on the lines north and south of Deraa, which are crucial to the Turks, while the main British offensive develops.

23 September
The Turkish garrison at Ma'an vacates the town, having been under siege since April, and surrenders to British forces on 28 September.

27 September
A Turkish force destroys the village of Tafas and kills the majority of its inhabitants in an act of reprisal. This Turkish force is later destroyed by elements of the Arab Army under Nuri as-Sa'id and Lawrence, aided by Pisani and his artillery. While accounts of this incident vary greatly, it would appear that few, if any, Turkish prisoners are taken.

28 September
The British 4th Cavalry Division under General Barrow and an advance party of the Arab army arrive in Deraa at the same time. Barrow finds tribesmen killing the wounded on a Turkish hospital train in the station.

1 October
Leading elements of the Arab Army, the 5th Cavalry Division and the Australian Mounted Division enter Damascus. Thereafter, the Arab Army continues to parallel the British advance northwards.

26 October
When the British Army enters Aleppo, it finds an Arab force already there.

29 October
British and regular troops of the Arab Army arrive at Muslimiya Junction, north of Aleppo. This crucial railway junction controls the Turkish rail link to the Mesopotamian front.

31 October
The Ottoman Empire is granted an armistice, ending the war in the Middle East.

1919

January
Having held out for another two months, Fakhri Pasha, the Ottoman commander of Medina, finally surrenders.

July
Lawrence and Pisani accompany Feisal to the Paris Peace Conference. In July 1919, Feisal is forced to leave Syria on the orders of the new French administration.

1921
A Middle East settlement is arrived at during the Cairo Conference. Under the terms of the British mandate, Feisal is to become king of Iraq (former Mesopotamia) in 1921 while his brother, Abdullah ibn Hussein, becomes king of Transjordan in 1923.

OPPOSING COMMANDERS

The Emir Feisal ibn Hussein, the third son of Sharif Hussein of Mecca. This charismatic figure emerged as the leader of the Arab Northern Army and would eventually lead it in its march to Damascus. (IWM Q58877)

ARAB COMMANDERS

Ali ibn Hussein (1853–1931) was the originator and the spiritual leader of the Arab Revolt that broke out against Ottoman rule in June 1916. In 1908 he had been appointed as the emir of the holy city of Mecca by the Ottoman sultan. Influenced by nationalistic trends among the Arab peoples, he had decided to begin negotiations with the British command in Cairo in early 1914, before war had even broken out. He established links with the al-Fatat movement in Damascus in early 1915. Following the outbreak of the revolt in 1916, he was proclaimed first as the 'king of the Arab lands' and then later as the 'king of the Hejaz'. He would abdicate in favour of his eldest son, Ali ibn Hussein, in 1924. Owing to the expansion of Saudi power into the Hejaz in 1925 he fled and ended his life in exile. Numerous Allied officials and officers, including Lawrence, later commented on Hussein's considerable abilities as a political leader and motivator of the revolt.

While Hussein acted as titular leader of the Arab Revolt, his sons served as military leaders in the field. His eldest son, the **Emir Ali ibn Hussein**, served as the leader of the Arab Southern Army and opposed the main Ottoman force at Medina throughout the war. Lawrence commented on his religious zeal and intelligence and he especially impressed the head of the French mission, Colonel Brémond. He was displaced as ruler of the Hejaz by the forces of Ibn Saud in 1925.

The **Emir Abdullah ibn Hussein** (1882–1951) commanded the Arab Eastern Army and campaigned against both the Ottoman Army and the forces of Ibn Saud, the great rivals of the Hashemite dynasty in Arabia. Prince Abdullah had also served as his father's emissary to the British command in Cairo in 1914 and had met with Lord Kitchener. Lawrence found him too politically sophisticated and strong willed to suit British purposes and it seems apparent that Abdullah was a formidable and unshakeable leader of the Hashemite cause. He acted as his father's Foreign Minister and was later recognized by the British as the king of Transjordan (modern-day Jordan).

It was, however, Hussein's third son, the **Emir Feisal ibn Hussein** (1886–1933), who emerged as the most prominent Arab leader of the revolt, at least from the perspective of later Western historians. He was identified early on by Allied officers as being an inspirational leader and, owing to his own ambitions was, perhaps more easy to direct. Lawrence first met him in October 1916 and felt that he best suited the Allied plans, which in reality meant that he was less intractable than his elder brothers. Feisal became the favourite Arab leader of

TOP LEFT

Architects of rebellion. Some of the main figures behind the Arab Revolt at a meeting in Jiddah in October 1916. The Emir Abdullah ibn Hussein is seated centre. Standing, left to right, are Said Bey, a former Arab officer in the Ottoman Army, Colonel Cyril Wilson, former British Governor of the Sudan, Aziz al-Masri, another former Ottoman officer, and Ronald Storrs of the British High Commission in Cairo. (IWM Q58706)

TOP RIGHT

Auda abu Tayi, seated second from right, the hereditary chief of the warlike Howeitat tribe. T. E. Lawrence took this photograph in 1921 at Amman in modern-day Jordan. Also included in this photo are, seated left to right, Auda ibn Zaal, Mohammed abu Tayi (Auda's son), an unknown tribesman and, to Auda's right, Zaal ibn Motlog, Auda's nephew. (IWM Q60169)

Lawrence, who encouraged him to seek power in Syria. He took command of the Arab Northern Army and led it northwards, greatly facilitated by the capture of Aqaba in 1917. Closely aligned with Lawrence, his army cooperated with General Allenby's forces during the final campaigns of 1918. Feisal's great skill was in motivating and uniting the Arab tribes under his command, while he also maintained the momentum of the Arab northern campaign.

Arab officers who had previously served in the Ottoman Army commanded the units of the Arab Regular Army. These men included some very able officers, such as **Jafar Pasha al-Askari** (1885–1936), a Kurd from Mesopotamia and a former Ottoman officer. He had undergone training in Germany and had played a major role in the Senussi Revolt of 1916, before being captured by the British. At the outbreak of the Arab Revolt he was a POW in Cairo but was eventually persuaded to join and lead the Arab Regular Army. He joined the campaign in 1917 and immediately displayed his tactical and administrative experience. Jafar Pasha was also an extremely tough and pragmatic commander, at one point advocating the use of mustard gas during the siege of Ma'an in 1918.

One of the first former Ottoman officers to serve the Arab cause was **Aziz Ali al-Masri,** a Circassian from Egypt who had also served in the Senussi Revolt before being persuaded to join the Arab cause. He joined the Arab forces in July 1916 and was an advocate of guerrilla warfare. Al-Masri recommended the formation of a 'flying column', which could then be used against the railway and also to push northwards into Syria. In fact, this was exactly what Feisal and Lawrence would later do. He was appointed as commander of the Arab Regular Army in 1916 but al-Masri was not popular with Hussein, who viewed the former Ottoman officers with some suspicion, and he was later sacked, being replaced by Jafar Pasha. As the first commander of the Sharifian Army, al-Masri was in reality the founding father of that army yet he has been largely forgotten by history.

Nuri as-Sa'id (1888–1958) was also a former Ottoman officer and in 1916 he commanded the regular troops of Prince Ali's Southern Arab Army. A talented artillery officer, he later served as chief of staff of the Arab Northern Army and served under Jafar Pasha.

The irregular forces of the Arab armies consisted of tribesmen who were commanded by their tribal chiefs. These included many leaders who showed a natural talent for guerrilla warfare. Perhaps the most famous of these was **Auda abu Tayi** (*c.*1870–1924), the hereditary chieftain of the Howeitat tribe and a close associate of Lawrence. He commanded the warlike tribesmen of the Abu Tayi branch of the Howeitat who were concentrated near Ma'an. His support was seen as being crucial by both sides and the Turks courted him throughout the war, even after he had proclaimed for the Hashemite cause and despite having previously been outlawed for killing two tax collectors. In a campaign in which larger-than-life figures seem to have abounded, Auda still stands out as a dramatic and charismatic leader, claiming to have killed 75 Arabs and countless Turks by his own hand in battle. There were numerous other tribal leaders who also played a major role in the revolt but have been largely forgotten. These included Sharif Nasir, who took part in the attack on Aqaba in 1917 and was also at the action at Tafila in 1918. He rose to command the irregular force of the Northern Arab Army. It is impossible in the space of this volume to enumerate the many other tribal leaders who played a part in ending Ottoman power in Arabia.

It must be pointed out that there were other Arab forces operating in Arabia that were not aligned with the Hashemite cause. **Abdul Aziz ibn Saud** (1880–1953) was also supported by the British and was a very capable military leader. He was the sultan of Najd in central Arabia and also controlled the coastal region of al Hasa. Ibn Saud numbered among his supporters members of the puritanical Wahabi sect, and during the war he opposed Ottoman forces and also pro-Ottoman tribes. He would emerge in the post-war years as a major force in Arabia and would eventually thwart Hashemite plans.

Some Arab tribes also remained loyal to the Ottomans. The most significant of these were the Shammar tribes, led by **Ibn Rashid**. Ibn Rashid effectively controlled north central Arabia with his power base at Ha'il. The Ottoman administration provided him with over 12,000 rifles and money and, while not incredibly active during the war, his forces acted as an effective counterbalance to both the Hashemite armies and also those of Ibn Saud. For the Arab Revolt, the very existence of this pro-Ottoman force had strategic implications and obliged the Hashemites to keep troops in the south to counter it.

General Sir Edmund Allenby, commander of the Egyptian Expeditionary Force from June 1917. He recognized the military potential of the Arab Revolt against the Ottomans and facilitated the Arab leaders so that their forces could play a major role in his campaigns to capture Palestine and Syria. (IWM Q82969)

ALLIED COMMANDERS

The British

At the outbreak of the Arab Revolt in 1916, the commander of the Egyptian Expeditionary Force was **General Sir Archibald Murray** (1860–1945), who had begun the war as chief of staff to the BEF in France. Having suffered from a stress-induced nervous breakdown he had become C-in-C Egypt in 1916. For the first year of its existence, therefore, the Arab Revolt relied on his patronage for arms, money and also men, either in the shape of British Army officers or Egyptian troops.

Murray's role in the history of the revolt has been the focus of much criticism and he is often portrayed as a hidebound, unimaginative general.

British officers and Arab tribesmen took part in operations against the Hejaz Railway before Lawrence arrived on the scene. Here Colonel Stewart Newcombe, second from left, Major al-Masri, second from right, and Lieutenant Hornby during a raid of 1917. (IWM Q58912)

There were mitigating factors to his behaviour, however. He has been criticized for his unwillingness to send troops to aid the revolt, yet it must be pointed out that his command was constantly being stripped of forces for the Western Front. His progress through Sinai has been derided for its snail-like pace but, at the same time, Murray was hampered by huge logistical difficulties and the apparent stagnation of British strategy was as a result of these problems – problems that he went to huge efforts to rectify. In ideological terms, it must be said that Murray disliked 'sideshows'. This dislike had a sound basis as he had seen sideshows like the Gallipoli and Mesopotamia campaigns descend into failure. These failures had always been achieved at great cost. Moreover, he had a profound distrust of the amateur officers, political officers and Arabists who seemed determined to initiate another sideshow in Arabia. Having failed in two successive battles at Gaza, Murray was replaced in June 1917.

Murray's successor was **General Sir Edmund Allenby** (1861–1936). Allenby has emerged from World War I as one of the great heroes of British arms. He had seen service in the Second Anglo-Boer War of 1899–1902 and in 1914 served with the BEF in France as GOC of the Cavalry Division. In 1915 he was given command of the Third Army but his later career on the Western Front was extremely mixed. After what was considered to be a poor performance at the battle of Arras in April 1917, he was removed from command. In June 1917 he was appointed to command the Egyptian Expeditionary Force.

Allenby's appointment came at a crucial time for the EEF, which had been demoralized owing to the failures of recent campaigns. He reorganized his force and restored morale. Allenby also recognized the potential of the Arab Revolt as both a means of tying down Ottoman troops in Arabia but also perhaps as a way of harassing the enemy by sending raids behind the Turkish left flank. His enthusiasm for the revolt was confirmed by Lawrence's capture of Aqaba, which occurred in July 1917, just after he had taken command. Allenby encouraged Feisal and Lawrence to take the revolt northwards and also supplied the Arab Army with armoured cars and air support. The success of the Arab army in 1917 and 1918 justified his support.

Three of the prime movers behind the Arab campaign in Palestine and Syria meet for tea at Wadi Quntilla in August 1917. Seated centre are Jafar Pasha al-Askari, the Emir Feisal and Colonel Pierce C. Joyce. Jafar Pasha was a former Ottoman officer who commanded the Arab Regular army from 1917. Joyce, a colonel in the Connaught Rangers who had been serving in Egypt since 1907, was commanding officer of Operation *Hedgehog*, the British military mission to the Arab Northern Army. (IWM Q59011)

In the months that followed the outbreak of the revolt, a number of other British officers were sent to Arabia to assist the Hashemite rebellion. The majority of them were serving in Arabia months before Lawrence had even left his desk in Cairo. In June 1916, **Colonel Cyril Wilson** (1873–1938), a former governor of the Sudan, was sent from Cairo under the cover of acting as a 'pilgrimage officer'. He headed the British mission at Jiddah and supervised the landing of military supplies while also liaising with the Hashemite leaders.

Another senior officer with the British mission was **Colonel Pierce C. Joyce** (1878–1965), who was a veteran of the Boer War and had been serving on the staff in Cairo since 1907. Joyce took command of the British base at Rabegh in December 1916 and would later command at Aqaba. From there he became the main organizer of logistical arrangements for Lawrence's expeditions into Palestine and Syria. Joyce was later appointed as head of the British military mission to the Arab Northern Army, codenamed Operation *Hedgehog*.

There were many other British officers who served in the initial stages of the revolt. They included **Colonel Stewart Francis Newcombe** (1878–1956), an officer with the Royal Engineers who had been associated with Lawrence before the war when he undertook a survey of the Sinai. Newcombe recognized the importance of the Hejaz Railway and embarked on a series of raids against the railway, before being captured by the Turks in October 1917. A whole cast of other officers served in the campaign between 1916 and 1918. To name them all would necessitate an exhaustive list.

To a certain extent, all of those who took part in the revolt, whether Arabs or Allied officers, have been overshadowed by **Thomas Edward (T. E.) Lawrence** (1888–1935). His actions in the war, and his post-war fame, have resulted in his becoming a modern legend. Born in 1888 in Wales, he was one of five illegitimate sons born to Sir Thomas Chapman, an Anglo-Irish baronet, and Ms Sarah Lawrence. He was educated at Jesus College, Oxford, and received a first-class degree, having travelled extensively in the Middle East for his BA dissertation on Crusader castles. Between 1911 and 1914 he

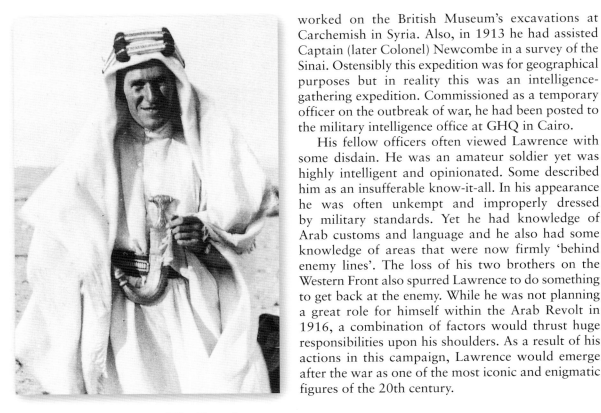

worked on the British Museum's excavations at Carchemish in Syria. Also, in 1913 he had assisted Captain (later Colonel) Newcombe in a survey of the Sinai. Ostensibly this expedition was for geographical purposes but in reality this was an intelligence-gathering expedition. Commissioned as a temporary officer on the outbreak of war, he had been posted to the military intelligence office at GHQ in Cairo.

His fellow officers often viewed Lawrence with some disdain. He was an amateur soldier yet was highly intelligent and opinionated. Some described him as an insufferable know-it-all. In his appearance he was often unkempt and improperly dressed by military standards. Yet he had knowledge of Arab customs and language and he also had some knowledge of areas that were now firmly 'behind enemy lines'. The loss of his two brothers on the Western Front also spurred Lawrence to do something to get back at the enemy. While he was not planning a great role for himself within the Arab Revolt in 1916, a combination of factors would thrust huge responsibilities upon his shoulders. As a result of his actions in this campaign, Lawrence would emerge after the war as one of the most iconic and enigmatic figures of the 20th century.

T. E. Lawrence in flowing Arab robes, as most readers imagine him, photographed at Aqaba in 1917. Lawrence was a relative latecomer to the Arab Revolt but the former archaeologist and intelligence officer would emerge as the most charismatic and memorable figure in the campaign. (IWM Q59314)

The French

In the months that followed the revolt, the French also established a military mission in order to aid the Arab cause. This was officially termed the 'Military Mission to Egypt' and had its base at Port Said, with the first members of the mission arriving in Alexandria in September 1916. At its height, the French mission numbered almost 1,100 officers and men.

The original commander of the French mission was **Colonel Edouard Brémond**, an officer of considerable experience who had campaigned in North Africa before commanding an infantry battalion on the Western Front. He was aided in his work by a number of other experienced officers and together they built up a healthy working relationship with Sharif Hussein and also his sons, emirs Ali and Abdullah. For this reason, most of the French effort was focused on the southern campaign around Mecca and Medina.

To some extent, the French had a considerable advantage over the British in that they could field Muslim officers from their North African regiments. These included **Colonel Cadi** and **Capitaine Muhammad Ould Ali Raho** (1877–1919). Capitaine Raho, of the 2e Régiment de Spahis Aljérien was an officer of vast experience. Having enlisted as a trooper in 1896, by 1903 he had served in 15 campaigns in North Africa. Raho was one of the first Allied officers to carry out missions against the Hejaz Railway, carrying out such a mission in February 1917. The French mission also included **Capitaine Laurnet Depui**, a hero of Verdun who later converted to Islam, and **Adjutant Claude Prost**, who became Sharif Hussein's foster brother.

The French officer who achieved the greatest prominence in the revolt was **Capitaine Rosario Pisani**, who was attached to the Arab Northern Army. Pisani originally operated with a small party of engineers and carried out attacks on the railway. He later commanded an artillery battery and accompanied Lawrence on some of the later campaigns of 1917 and 1918. A close associate of Feisal, he would later support the Arab cause at the Paris Peace Conference of 1919.

Finally, it must also be pointed out that, because of the long-term implications of this campaign, there were a number of political officials of both the British and the French governments who were involved closely with efforts to direct the revolt. These ranged from senior civil servants such as Sir Mark Sykes and Georges Picot, to local officials such as Sir Reginald Wingate, Governor of the Sudan. Other political figures who played an important role were Sir Henry McMahon, British High Commissioner in Egypt, and Ronald Storrs. The policies devised by such men would have a direct bearing on the conduct of the campaign.

Colonel Brémond, commanding officer of the French mission to the Hejaz. He had considerable experience of desert warfare in North Africa and had recently served as a corps chief of staff on the Western Front. (Bailloud collection, Service Historique de la Défense, Vincennes)

OTTOMAN COMMANDERS

The most senior Ottoman officer in the campaign against the Arab Revolt was **Mehmed Cemal Pasha, 'Büyük'** (1872–1922). He had been an early member of the Young Turk movement and on the outbreak of war was a senior figure in the government, holding the office of Minister of Marine. During the war, he held two other senior military offices alongside his ministry. He was military governor of Ottoman Syria and as such had been responsible for the crackdown against Arab nationalists in the first years of the war. As governor, his responsibility included Palestine and stretched as far as Arabia. Cemal Pasha was also the commander of the Ottoman Fourth Army and had been the instigator of the unsuccessful attack on the Suez Canal in February 1915. A highly intelligent and somewhat ruthless commander, he forbade the withdrawal of troops from Arabia.

In Arabia itself, the most senior commander was **General Hamid Fakhreddin ('Fakhri') Pasha** (1868–1948). An officer of considerable experience and ability, he became the de facto supreme commander in Arabia as he commanded the largest and most effective force from Medina. Like Cemal Pasha he held dual rules, acting both as governor of Medina and military commander. His defence of Medina was inspired and he tied down two of the three Arab armies for much of the war.

It is difficult to get a true sense of the performance of the other Ottoman commanders in the field due to the lack of Turkish sources in English. It must also be said that many English-language sources often pay little attention to these men. It can be seen, however, that officers such as **Mehmed Cemal Pasha (Küçük or Üçüncü)**, the commanding officer of the 1st Kuvve-i Mürettebe, which was responsible for railway security, carried out their duties commendably despite the difficulties they faced in trying to counter a campaign of railway sabotage in a theatre that covered a vast area.

OPPOSING ARMIES

THE ARAB ARMY

The Hashemite Army that instigated the Arab Revolt was composed of tribesmen from both the settled and nomadic Arab tribes. It is difficult to get an accurate assessment of how large this army was. Some estimates suggest 30,000 tribesmen who took part in the initial actions around Mecca, Medina and Ta'if.

Not all of these tribesmen matched the stereotype that is held in the west of dashing, camel-mounted warriors. Many of the first followers of Sharif Hussein and his sons were from the highlands of the Hejaz. They were simple farmers, often impoverished, whose harsh rural existence hardened them for life on campaign.

Further tribesmen joined from the nomadic tribes and, as the campaign became more mobile, they played an increasingly important role. To give a full listing of all the nomadic tribes that joined the revolt would be impossible in the scope of this volume. They included tribesmen of the Harith, the Bani 'Ali, the Bani 'Atiya, the Bani Salem, the Juhaynah, the Utaybah and the Howeitat among many others. In geographical terms, their tribal heartlands spanned a large area from the southern Hejaz as far northwards as modern-day Jordan. As the campaign moved into Palestine and Syria in 1917 and

The Emir Feisal leads his army into Yanbu in December 1916. The possession of ports on the Red Sea allowed the Royal Navy to supply the revolt and also provide artillery and air support. (IWM Q58754)

An atmospheric photograph of the Arab camp at Nakhl Mubarak near Yanbu. Lawrence took this photograph in January 1917. During the last months of 1916, this camp served as Feisal's main base for his defence against approaching Turkish forces. (IWM Q58838)

1918, tribesmen were recruited from these areas. Later recruits included Arab farmers of the Hauran area and also men from the Christian minorities.

Using such men to engage in a guerrilla war against the Ottomans made eminent good sense as for centuries tribal warfare had essentially been guerrilla warfare. The men of the Arab irregular army could cover vast distances on camelback and then dismount to fight on foot. They could survive in areas where survival was thought to be impossible. The Arab irregulars also proved to be excellent shots, especially as they were increasingly re-armed with modern rifles.

There were also disadvantages in using these men. They were untrained and often lacked discipline. In raids on Ottoman positions, they excelled, but they could not be used, in general, in major offensive or defensive actions. Many were reluctant to move outside their own tribal areas, which meant that, as the campaign moved northwards, new followers had to be recruited and paid. The payment of the irregular army represented a huge investment on the part of the Allied governments. Payment had to be in gold coin, which was shipped across the Red Sea. By the end of 1916, the French Government had spent 1.25 million gold francs in Arabia. By that stage, the monthly allowance to support the Emir Feisal's Arab Northern Army cost the British £30,000 in gold coin. By September 1918, the monthly British allowance to the Hashemite cause was £220,000.

At the outbreak of the revolt, it also became apparent that these tribesmen would have to be entirely re-armed. While the British command in Egypt had sent some weapons across the Red Sea before the outbreak of the revolt, it would appear that the majority of tribesmen were still armed with muzzle-loading jazail muskets. In the short term, a re-arming programme got under way using captured Ottoman weapons and also a quantity of Japanese Arisaka rifles supplied by the British. Later in the campaign an effort was made to supply all tribesmen with a British service rifle, usually the excellent Short Magazine Lee Enfield (SMLE) in .303in. The widespread issue of this weapon increased the effectiveness and firepower of the Arab irregulars and also made it easier for the British to supply both ammunition and spare parts. Nevertheless, in some late 1918 photographs it can be seen that the tribesmen were still using different types of rifle, so re-supply with the SMLE never reached all of the irregulars. Other photographs show Arab tribesmen with long Lee Enfield rifles.

The Arab irregulars were also issued with support weapons. It was thought that their style of warfare negated the use of heavy weapons, so they were issued with light machine guns only. These included both the French Hotchkiss and the British Lewis gun, both of which fell into the 'light machine gun' category. The larger Vickers or Maxim guns would not seem to have been generally issued, which probably made sense as they were heavier weapons that used tripods and water-cooling systems. They would not have been easy to transport and the water-cooling system presented obvious problems in a desert campaign. Nevertheless, Lawrence mentions their use by tribesmen during the Tafila action of January 1918.

While the Arab Regular Army, which will be discussed below, wore a uniform, the irregulars retained their own Arab clothing. This made eminent good sense as these clothes were suitable for camel riding and life in the desert, both factors that played a part in the life of tribal irregulars. As headdress they wore the Arab keffiyah head cloth and they also wore loose cotton trousers, Arab cloaks (aba) and also tunics or the dishdashah, an ankle-length garment in loose cotton. Colours of these garments would differ from tribe to tribe, creating a very non-uniform appearance when different tribal groupings campaigned together.

Within the tribal irregulars, a specific contingent deserves special mention. These tribesmen came from the Agayl, who formed a distinct warrior class in Arab society. The Agayl had their homeland in the Hejaz and the Najd regions and were predominantly settled tribesmen. They were famous as camel-traders and as such their young men travelled throughout Arabia. They also had a tradition of working as mercenaries and enjoyed a considerable reputation as camel-mounted warriors. They played an invaluable part in the Arab Revolt. As mercenaries, they were willing to travel outside of their tribal homelands and as a result these experienced desert fighters travelled with the Arab Northern Army as it moved northwards. They were particularly valued among the Hashemite leaders and many were recruited into personal bodyguards: Lawrence himself later recruited from among the Agayl for his own bodyguard.

While the irregular tribal contingent was excellent for guerrilla warfare, it was recognized early on that a regular force would also have to be raised to provide a hard core of fighters for the Arab Revolt. This force came to known as the Regular Arab Army or the Sharifian Army. At the outbreak of the revolt there was a source of recruits close at hand as the British had captured thousands of Ottoman soldiers in campaigns in Sinai, Libya and also Mesopotamia. These Ottoman POWs included Arab officers and soldiers. Many of the officers, who included men of Iraqi or Syrian birth, were sympathetic to the Arab cause. Among the enlisted men there were also men of Arab birth. In late 1916, the first 1,000 men were sent to the Hejaz and these men formed the first detachment of the Sharifian Army. They were experienced, trained, disciplined soldiers and as such they played a major part in the revolt, taking part in several conventional actions such as the attacks around Ma'an in April 1918.

While there were Regular Army contingents with all the Arab armies, it was with the Arab Northern Army that they were most numerous. In this army they numbered around 2,000 men, all ranks. The infantry was formed into two main units, alternatively referred to as 'divisions' or 'brigades'. The infantry numbered around 1,500–1,600 men and they were supported by a camel corps, mule-mounted infantry, artillery and also machine-gun detachments. They were armed with SMLE rifles and given standard British uniforms but wore an Arab keffiyah headdress rather than British headgear.

The lack of artillery dogged all the Arab armies but especially the Arab Northern Army throughout the campaign. The amount of available artillery was never adequate. Some Turkish mountain guns were captured at Ta'if at the beginning of the campaign and to these the British added some obsolete artillery from the Egyptian Army. The French supplied both a field and a mountain battery, and further Turkish guns were captured at Tafila in early 1918. Yet the lack of modern artillery hampered the operations of the Arab Northern Army. Machine guns were, however, supplied in large numbers and, as was the case with the irregular contingent, these were of the Hotchkiss and Lewis types and also the heavier Vickers gun.

The Arab armies contained therefore both irregular and regular units. From its inception, the revolt also had a European contingent made up of British and French personnel. Initially the Allied powers were represented by an officer contingent that acted as political officers, training officers and who also controlled the supply of material. Engineering officers helped improve the defences of the towns that were held by Hashemite forces. While such activities were continued throughout the war, British and French officers began to pay an increasingly important role. They took part in the campaign against the railway and soon European NCOs were also training Arab troops in the use of light machine guns, artillery and Stokes mortars. The French had a training mission based at Mecca, made up of Muslim officers and NCOs from North Africa, while British officers fulfilled the same role with the Arab Northern Army.

By late 1917, the European contingent had increased considerably. The British Army had supplied the Arab Northern Army with a squadron of Rolls-Royce armoured cars and also Talbot cars, some of which mounted 10-pdr guns. A flight of aircraft had been attached. Initially these were of obsolescent BE2s but later some of the excellent Bristol F2 Fighters were attached to the northern force. The addition of such units increased the military potential of the Arab Northern Army and they played an important role in the later campaigns of the war.

The use of European troops en masse remained a difficult point, as the Hashemite leaders did not want to be seen using infidel western troops in their campaign. Even Allied officers recognized the sensitivities of sending European troops to campaign in the most holy region of the Muslim world. In the early months of the revolt, the British sent Egyptian troops as a means of circumventing this issue while the French could rely on Muslim troops of their own. Later troops from the Indian Army would serve alongside the Arab Northern Army and these would include Gurkhas. In 1918 a force of the Imperial Camel Corps (raised from British yeomanry units) was also added. By the end of the war, therefore, it could be argued that the Arab Northern Army was one of the most cosmopolitan forces to take part in the war.

THE OTTOMAN ARMY

There is a common misconception that the Ottoman Army of World War I was entirely 'propped up' by German forces. There had indeed been a huge pre-war reform of the Ottoman Army and the influence of the German military mission of General Liman von Sanders was significant, both in the re-equipping of the army and in its training. German influence has been greatly exaggerated and nowhere is this more true than on the Arabian front where German influence was minimal.

It is also assumed that the Ottoman Army in Arabia was on the verge of collapse for much of the war. But it can be shown that new formations were raised and that the Turkish Army was capable of offensive operations in Arabia for much of the war. At its height the Ottoman Army in Arabia numbered over 20,000 men. This force was formed into conventional divisions and also composite units that were formed to react against the Arab Revolt in general and also attacks on the railway in particular. They were supported by artillery, cavalry, mule-mounted infantry and other logistical and medical units. The Ottoman gendarmerie also provided a useful auxiliary force and could be used for garrison duties while the Ottoman camel-mounted infantry was found to be particularly effective. At the beginning of the campaign, some planes of the Ottoman Air Force were rushed to the Hejaz. These would later be supported by further planes from the Ottoman and German air forces. They had considerable effect when used against tribal forces.

The individual Turkish soldier had proved his worth in a series of campaigns before 1916. While at the beginning of the war Allied officers had not rated Turkish troops highly, they had since been forced to revise this opinion radically. The campaigns in Gallipoli and Mesopotamia in particular illustrated the fighting qualities and tenacity of the Turkish infantryman, or 'Johnny Turk' as he came to be known. Attitudes to the Ottoman officer corps had also been revised in light of these campaigns.

At the outbreak of the war, the VIII Corps of the Ottoman Fourth Army defended Arabia, but in the prelude to the outbreak of the revolt further Ottoman troops had been sent southwards to Medina. In response to the revolt, new formations were raised, including the 58th Infantry Division, under Lieutenant-Colonel Ali Necib Pasha, the 1st Kuvve-i Mürettebe (Provisional Force) commanded by General Mehmed Cemal Pasha (Küçük) and the Hicaz Kuvvei Seferiyesi ('Expeditionary Force of the Hejaz') commanded by General Fakhri Pasha. These new formations were based at Ma'an and Medina and were tasked with keeping the railway open and also operating against the Arab armies. The 2nd Kuvve-i Mürettebe had been raised by 1917 and was based at Tabuk.

The composition of the Ottoman Army in Arabia was also interesting as it contained several Arab units. While both the Hejaz and the Najd regions were exempt from military conscription, large numbers of Arabs fought with the Ottoman Army on all fronts, including Arabia. There is no indication that these Arab units were prone to higher rates of desertion.

The great difficulty for the Ottoman commanders in Arabia was one of supply. Owing to the limited infrastructure in this vast area, a great reliance was placed on the Hejaz Railway. Road networks were not good and transport equipment was less than adequate. This placed huge limitations on the Ottoman commanders and it can be shown that a number of expeditions against the Arabs ended prematurely because of logistical problems rather than enemy opposition. The re-supply and re-equipping of Ottoman units was therefore uneven throughout the war. By the end of the war, it was becoming increasingly difficult to re-equip and re-clothe troops on all fronts and shortages became especially acute in Arabia. Nevertheless, Ottoman troops continued to give a good account of themselves until the end of the war in Arabia and, in some cases, even beyond that.

For Ottoman troops, the Arab Revolt could mean operating in the field with one of the larger formations sent out against the Arabs. In many cases it meant long periods spent on garrison duty. If the soldier was lucky, this was in one of the large centres of Ottoman power such as Ma'an. It could also mean long and dangerous periods of garrison duty in blockhouses along the Hejaz Railway. Ottoman soldiers' weapons could include any one of a number of rifles from the Turkish Mauser models M1893 and M1903 to German Mauser M1898. Some troops were issued with obsolete rifles such as the Turkish Mauser M1887. Despite these potential shortcomings, the Ottoman Army was to perform well owing largely to the military qualities and inherent tenaciousness of its officers and men. It must also be pointed out, however, that the Ottoman reaction to revolt was often robust, to say the least. Accounts of the massacre of civilians are still much debated but it would seem to be true that Ottoman soldiers engaged in reprisals on several occasions during the revolt.

ORDERS OF BATTLE

THE ARAB ARMY 1916–18

The original Arab force that instigated the revolt between 5 and 10 June 1916 consisted of up to 30,000 Arab tribesmen who rose in revolt at Medina and Mecca.

Late 1916

9,000 men under the Emir Ali, located south of Medina
8,000 men under the Emir Feisal, encamped near Yanbu
1,500 Egyptian troops and irregulars sent by the British

The Arab Northern Army, 1917–18

Commander: The Emir Feisal ibn Hussein
Deputy Commander: The Emir Zeid ibn Hussein

The Regular Sharifian Army (around 2,000 men)
Commander: Jafar Pasha al-Askari
Chief of staff: Nuri as-Sa'id
    1st Division (Aqaba) – Brig. Gen. Amin al-Asil
        Hashemite Infantry Brigade (two battalions of around 400 men each)
    2nd Division (Quwayra) – Lt. Col. Majid Hasun
        Hashemite Infantry Brigade (800)
An artillery contingent of eight guns crewed by 150 men and commanded by Rasim Sardast
A machine-gun detachment, commanded by Abdullah Al-Dulaimi
A battalion of the Hejaz Camel Corps, commanded by Khalid Sa'id
Mule-mounted infantry originally commanded by Maulud al-Mukhlis
Associated logistical and medical units.

The Irregular Army/Tribal Forces
Around 6,000 tribesmen from various tribes including the Howeitat, the Bani 'Ali, the Bali, the Juhaynah, the Utaybah, among others. Commanded by their own tribal chiefs including Auda abu Tayi, Sharif Nasir ibn Ali, Sharif Ali ibn Arayd and Sharif Mastur, among others.

The Arab Southern Army, 1916–18

Based at Rabegh and commanded by the Emir Ali ibn Hussein, this force opposed the Turkish forces at Medina. It consisted of:
2 x infantry battalions
1 x battalion mule-mounted infantry
1 x battalion of camel-mounted infantry
4 x artillery batteries
1 x engineer company
A contingent of tribal forces

The Arab Eastern Army, 1916–18

This army was commanded by the Emir Abdullah ibn Hussein and it operated against the pro-Ottoman Shammar tribe.
It consisted of:
2 x battalions of camel-mounted infantry
1 x cavalry squadron
1 x battery of mountain artillery
A contingent of Hashemite volunteers
A contingent of tribal irregular forces

Operation *Hedgehog*: the British Military Mission to the Arab Northern Army, 1916–18

Colonel P. C. Joyce commanding until March 1918. From March 1918, Colonel Alan Dawney
This force included Stokes mortar and machine-gun crews attached from the British and Indian Armies. There were also Egyptian troops, Gurkhas and a labour corps. In 1918 a company of over 300 men of the Imperial Camel Corps was also attached.
The force also contained:
The Hejaz Armoured Car Company, consisting of Rolls-Royce armoured cars
The Hejaz Talbot Car Battery, consisting of Talbot cars, some of which were mounted with 10-pdr guns.

Air support:
From 1916, RFC/RAF planes were attached to this force as support. These initially consisted of 4 x BE2 aircraft. In 1918 they also included Bristol F2 Fighters.

French military mission to the Hejaz, 1916–18

Commanded by Colonel Edouard Brémond until December 1917
In October 1916 the French contingent included:
8 x Hotchkiss MG sections
1 x battery mountain guns (six guns)
1 x battery of field artillery (six guns)
1 x engineer company
1 x support company.

The French strength in March 1917 stood at 47 officers and 1,127 men based at Port Said, the majority of troops being drawn from units from French North Africa. There were also small detachments at Mecca and Rabegh.
The French force also contained a Régiment mixte de marche de Cavalerie, drawn from various cavalry regiments including the Algerian Spahi.

OTTOMAN FORCES IN THE HEJAZ, 1916–18

The Ottoman Army in Arabia was composed of troops from the Fourth Army.
Fourth Army – General Mehmed Cemal Pasha (Büyük) – 23,000 men
Chief of staff: Colonel Ali Faut Bey.
VIII Corps – General Mehmed Cemal Pasha (Mersinli)
    8th Infantry Division
    10th Infantry Division

23rd Infantry Division
25th Infantry Division
27th Infantry Division

Jiddah

Cidde Mufrezesi, June 1916
General Staff Major Huseyin Husn
1/128th Infantry Battalion
2/128th Infantry Battalion
1 x machine-gun company (four machine guns)
1 x mountain artillery battery (four guns)

Mecca

Mekke Kumandanl, June 1916
Major Ziya (captured on 11 June 1916)
General Staff Major Dervi (the chief of staff of the 22nd Infantry
Division, took over the command following Ziva's capture)
3/128th Infantry Battalion
2/130th Infantry Battalion
1 x infantry company, recruited locally from among former
Sudanese slaves.
2 x mountain artillery batteries (seven to eight guns)
Detachment gendarmerie.
Support company.

Ta'if

June 1916
General Ghalib, military governor and commanding officer
of the 22nd Infantry Division
Local military commander, Ahmad Bey of Mehmed Bey
Divisional staff and HQ elements
1/129th Infantry Battalion
3/129th Infantry Battalion
Gendarmerie battalion
2 x mountain gun batteries
Support elements (medical, logistical)

Railway protection army group based at Ma'an

1st Kuvve-i Mürettebe, late 1916
The title of this unit translates literally as 'provisional force'
It was administered by an army corps level HQ under the
command of General Mehmed Cemal Pasha (Küçük or Üçüncü).
This unit was founded to provide security for the Hejaz Railway
at the end of 1916. The HQ moved to El-Ala on 16 February 1917
but returned to Ma'an on 24 September 1917.
138th Infantry Regiment
161st Infantry Regiment
1/79th Infantry Battalion
One battery from the 6th Field Artillery Battalion
3 x cavalry squadrons
Ma'an Gendarmerie Battalion
2 x infantry companies (from 31st Infantry Regiment and
130th Infantry Regiment)

2 x railway companies
Circassian Volunteer Cavalry Regiment
Logistical and medical support elements
Units later attached to railway protection included the 23rd,
42nd 162nd and 178th infantry regiments

In 1917, the 2nd Kuvve-i Mürettebe was formed and based at Tabuk.

Hicaz Kuvve-i Seferiyesi

The title of this command organization translates literally as
'the expeditionary force of the Hejaz'. Its HQ was at Medina.
It was administered by a field army level HQ and was under the
command of General Fakhreddin (Fakhri) Pasha. It arrived at this
theatre of operations on 31 May 1916 and the chief of staff was
Lt. Col. Emin.
Hecins var Regiment (camel corps)
1st Aknc Regiment (volunteer Arab cavalry)
3 x field artillery batteries
2 x signal companies
Medical and logistical support elements

Medina Fortress Command

This unit was commanded by General Basri Pasha with Lt. Col.
Galib as second in command.
2nd Aknc Regiment
4/131st Infantry Battalion
2/129th Infantry Battalion
Gendarmerie Battalion
1 x railway battalion
2 x artillery batteries

58th Infantry Division

This division was founded on 28 October 1916 and was under
the command of Lt. Col. Ali Necib. The chief of staff was Major
Yusuf Ziya.
42nd Infantry Regiment
55th Infantry Regiment, commanded by Abderhaman Bey
130th Infantry Regiment
Esters var Battalion (mule-mounted infantry battalion)
1 x mountain artillery battery

Coastal garrisons

Aqaba 1916: 2 x companies gendarmerie
Aqaba 1917: elements of the 161st Infantry Regiment
Wejh 1916: elements of the 129th Infantry Regiment
Yanbu 1916: elements of the 45th and 129th Infantry Regiments
Southern Arabia/Yemen: VII Corps, consisting of the 21st, 22nd,
39th and 40th Infantry Divisions

Air Support

Following the outbreak of the revolt, 3 x Pfalz AII of the
Ottoman Air Force were shipped to the Hejaz. These were later
supplemented with further Ottoman and German planes.

OPPOSING PLANS

THE ARAB PLAN

The plan of the Hashemite leaders in 1916 was simple in principle but hugely difficult to execute. Their basic aim was to rid Arabia of both the Ottoman Army and the administration it supported. To complete this task would have required a large, disciplined army with a well-organized logistical supply network. It would also have required support among all of the tribes of Arabia. Sharif Hussein and the Hashemite leaders had none of these things and this led to huge difficulties at both the planning and operational levels of the revolt. These difficulties were compounded by problems in communications and also personality clashes within the Hashemite command. Ultimately, what they could plan for in the initial stages of the revolt was a limited operation with limited goals in mind.

There has been so much speculation and assumption made since 1916 about Arab intentions and it is sometimes difficult to assess just what was being planned for at the beginning of the revolt. But analysis of events can lead to conclusions about what the Arab leaders thought they could realistically achieve.

One of their first priorities in their planning had to be the taking of the holy cities of Mecca and Medina. While Sharif Hussein was the emir of Mecca, he needed to convert his currency as a spiritual leader into real political power. Medina, as the resting place of the Prophet Muhammad, was an equally important location. If the Hashemites held the two most important locations in Islam they could then be viewed as the de facto leaders of the Islamic religion.

Medina was also of strategic importance as it was the terminus of the Hejaz Railway. It connected Arabia with the nearest major centre of Ottoman administration in Damascus and from there back to Constantinople. It was the location of a large garrison and was also the location to which reinforcements would be sent. In military terms, therefore, Medina was of prime importance.

Ta'if also emerged in Hashemite plans as a major objective. In the summer months, the main garrison of Mecca was moved there to escape the worst of the heat during this season. In order to be certain of Mecca, the garrison at Ta'if had also to be attacked and neutralized.

Implicit in Arab plans was the hope that they would be further supported by Britain and perhaps France. For this to happen the coastal towns on the Red Sea also would have to be taken and Jiddah, Rabegh and Yanbu became objectives also. If these towns were secured, further military supplies could be

landed. In the worst-case scenario, they could be used as points of evacuation. Jiddah could serve Mecca while Rabegh and Yanbu were close to Medina.

From the beginning of the campaign, the Arabs were also aware of the importance of the Hejaz Railway. Indeed the importance of the railway to Turkish operations had long been recognized, one Turkish source claiming that attacks by Arab nationalists were not uncommon before 1914. As part of the plan for the revolt, the railway would have to be attacked and cut to prevent, or at least delay, Ottoman reinforcements being sent south into Arabia. The line north of Medina would be the target for such attacks.

The Hashemite plan was therefore both simple and elaborate. It required the simultaneous attack on a number of strategic locations. It required the seizing of ports and it required the interdiction of supplies and reinforcements along the Hejaz Railway. For a well-trained and disciplined force, this would have presented difficulties. It also meant that, rather than concentrating their forces, the Arab leaders had to dissipate them in a series of attacks over a wide area.

The failure to take Medina had serious strategic ramifications and these will be discussed later. Suffice to say that this had a major effect on future Arab plans as two Arab armies had to remain in the vicinity of Medina and Mecca to counter Turkish counterattacks from Medina. The fact that these Hashemite armies had to counter the forces of both Ibn Saud and Ibn Rashid also affected planning as it became imperative to hold these forces in the south to maintain Hashemite power in Mecca. From late 1916, therefore, retaining control of these parts of the Hejaz played a large part in Hashemite planning.

It is fitting at this point also to examine the plans of Prince Feisal and his Arab Northern Army. As the third son of Sharif Hussein it was made increasingly clear to him by his father and elder brothers after the outbreak of the revolt that he could expect little in any post-war settlement in Arabia. As a result of this, and encouraged by T. E. Lawrence, he looked northwards in the hope of giving scope to his ambitions. The hope of being able to

The Emir Feisal (in white head cloth and robes) leading his army towards Wejh in January 1917. Behind him, standard-bearers carry furled Hashemite banners. At the time, this was the largest tribal army in living memory. (IWM Q58863)

become ruler of Palestine or Syria prompted him to move northwards to Wejh and then Aqaba. For Feisal, the success of Allenby's campaigns in 1917 and 1918 was crucial for his own plans.

These forces underpinned the most dramatic phase of the Arab Revolt as the Arab Northern Army began to play a major part in British plans from the summer of 1917.

THE BRITISH PLAN

From June 1916, the Arab Revolt began to play a part in British plans. Depending on who was C-in-C in Egypt, these plans represented two very different strategic mindsets. Up to his replacement in June 1917, General Murray had a limited but perhaps realistic view of what the Arabs could do to support British plans. At the outbreak of the revolt, Murray's long-term strategy was to move the British Army through Sinai with the intention of both advancing into Palestine and pushing the Turks back from the Suez Canal Zone.

How could the Arabs aid this plan? For Murray they represented an untried and untrained force, but if supplied with military material they could become a nuisance to the Turks and thus hold down troops in Arabia – troops that would otherwise be used in Palestine. Ultimately, therefore, Murray saw them as having 'nuisance value' only and while he continued to send supplies to the Arabs he repeatedly refused to send troops. His vision was to limit the revolt to the Hejaz with the intention of holding Turkish troops in the Hejaz.

It was left to General Allenby to recognize the full potential of the Arab Revolt and see how it could be used to aid his long-term strategy for taking Palestine and Syria. As it was, the campaign in Arabia was indeed tying down large numbers of Ottoman troops. Following the capture of Aqaba in July 1917, Allenby sent more and more military *matériel* to Feisal's Arab Northern Army, recognizing that the attacks on the railway, and more general raiding, represented a massive return on his investment. Based on reports sent to Cairo by Lawrence and other senior British officers, he came to recognize that the Emir Feisal's hopes of advancing into Syria could fit nicely into his own plans. For this reason, the Arab Army based at Aqaba played a major part in British planning throughout 1917 and 1918. In future operations they would be used to divert the enemy, destroy his rail links and, in the final campaign of 1918, harass the Turkish left flank as Allenby advanced into Syria.

THE OTTOMAN PLAN

By 1916 the Ottoman Army had resisted attacks by Allied armies in Gallipoli, Mesopotamia and along its eastern borders with Russia. From June 1916, the Ottoman command had to deal with internal revolt in Arabia. The Turkish plan in Arabia from 1916 also developed in the two years that followed.

In its earliest form, Turkish plans were quite simple – this was a revolt that had to be suppressed and the captured towns had to be recaptured. The initial Turkish reaction was optimistic and it was felt that this could be achieved easily, demonstrated by the fact that a new emir of Mecca was appointed (Sharif Ali Haidar) and sent south to Medina. Realizing these plans would prove difficult.

The initial Ottoman countermoves failed to come to grips with the Arab enemy in order to destroy it. In the vast spaces of southern Arabia, the tribal enemy seemed to melt away. They did not offer battle in the classic sense and the Ottoman Army needed a large logistical system to maintain itself in the field.

The details of the Ottoman efforts to end the rebellion will be discussed later in the text. It is sufficient to point out here that, having failed to put it down in 1916, the main strategic concern became the garrison at Medina. By its very existence, it kept large Arab forces in the area. It also became the focus of a build-up of troops and the plan was that further decisive expeditions would later take place against the Arabs.

The crucial strategic consideration for the Turks came to be the Hejaz Railway. It had to be kept open so that the Medina garrison, and also lesser garrisons along the line, could survive. It had to be kept open to allow for the possibility of later military action. In short it was necessary for the Ottoman Army to survive in Arabia and for there to be any possibility for any re-establishment of Ottoman rule. Yet maintaining this line would occupy much of the time and resources of Turkish planners. While the Turks remained at Medina, they also represented the extreme left flank of the

The port of Wejh on the Red Sea. In moving his army northwards to this port, Feisal changed the direction of the revolt. (Bailloud collection, SHD, Vincennes)

Turkish line. This was a consideration for both Murray and Allenby as they made plans to push into Palestine as, regardless of how far any British force might advance, the garrison at Medina would still pose a threat as it constituted a large enemy force behind the British right, albeit at some considerable distance. Even when hampered by the cutting of the railway, such a large Turkish contingent in Arabia remained a factor in British planning.

Further to the south, the Ottoman Army maintained a division in the Yemen. While the history of the war in the Yemen cannot be examined here in any detail, it must be pointed out that the strategic situation demanded that Medina be retained. In light of the Royal Navy's control of the Red Sea, Medina represented the nearest source of practical aid for the garrison in the Yemen.

In Ottoman plans therefore, the maintenance of the railway line and the retention of Medina formed a major part of long-term strategy in Arabia.

THE POLITICAL PLAN

The plans of government officials also played a part in shaping the Arab Revolt. Decisions made in London and Paris, even before the revolt had broken out, had long-term ramifications for Arabia.

The imminent collapse of the Ottoman Empire had been predicted since the mid-19th century. Following Turkey's entry into the war government officials of the Entente powers began to discuss how Turkish territory should be divided after its defeat. Of course, these discussions in no way reflected military reality. While British and French forces were suffering defeats in Gallipoli and Mesopotamia, senior civil servants met to decide how former Ottoman territory would be ruled. The two most prominent officials in this process were Sir Mark Sykes for Britain and M. Georges Picot for France.

One of the iconic images of Lawrence. This photograph was taken by an unknown photographer sometime in 1917. (IWM Q60212)

Their negotiations continued throughout late 1915 and in February 1916 a broad agreement was reached. This agreement was ratified in May 1916 in what came to be known as the 'Sykes–Picot Agreement'. Under its terms, France would take control of Syria, Lebanon and Turkish Cilicia. Under its mandate, Britain was to control Mesopotamia, Transjordan and Palestine. Russia was to take control of the Armenian and Kurdish territories along Turkey's north-eastern border. The holy city of Jerusalem was to be governed by an international commission, while Arabia was to receive a certain level of independence.

These plans did not reflect the aspirations of the Arab peoples. Also, they did not reflect the promises later made by British and French officers on behalf of their governments. As Lawrence later put it, the Arabs were 'fighting for us on a lie'. As news of these political plans was leaked, they had a real impact on the Allied–Arab relationship and endangered the future of the Arab Revolt.

THE ARAB REVOLT

A street scene taken in Jiddah in 1916. (IWM Q58710)

THE OUTBREAK OF THE ARAB REVOLT, JUNE 1916

At first light on the morning of 10 June 1916, the call for prayer rang out from the minaret of the mosque in Mecca. This moment had been chosen by the Hashemite leader, Sharif Hussein ibn Ali, as the starting point for the revolt against Ottoman power in the Hejaz. As the call came to its end, he took a rifle and walked to the window of his house and fired a single shot. This was the signal for his supporters, who had come into the city in twos and threes the previous night, to go into action. A Hashemite flag fluttered to the flagpole above Sharif Hussein's house. The Arab Revolt had begun.

Despite the fact that the Ottoman high command in Damascus was expecting trouble and had even begun moving reinforcements into the region, the outbreak of the revolt seems to have taken the local commanders by surprise. In Mecca, the garrison was divided between the Jirwal Barracks on the Jiddah Road and also in the imposing Jiyad fortress. There was also a small garrison in the offices of the Ottoman governor. In total there were only 1,500 or so troops in Mecca as the majority of the garrison had been moved to Ta'if for the hot season.

The HQ of the French misson at Wejh. (Bailloud collection, SHD, Vincennes)

33

A day of confused street fighting followed and, while the garrison at the governor's offices surrendered the next day, the remaining garrison in both the barracks and the Jiyad fortress continued to defend themselves. With the benefit of both artillery and machine guns, they shut down the Arab attack. Stalemate ensued as the Ottoman commanders settled into a siege and awaited help from Medina. The Arabs, lacking artillery, could not press home attacks on the two main Turkish positions. It seemed as though the revolt might last only a few weeks, as it proved impossible to dislodge the Turks or force them to surrender. From the Turkish fortress shells were fired into the town. This caused much damage within the holy city for which the Turks were later criticized throughout the Islamic world.

This situation lasted into July until Egyptian troops and a mountain battery arrived at Mecca. These had been rushed across the Red Sea by the Royal Navy and were immediately put into action against the Jiyad fortress. The fortress's walls were breached and the garrison surrendered. The Egyptian gunners then turned their attention on the Turkish barracks and their shells started a fire there. Lacking enough water to put the fire out, the last of the garrison surrendered on 9 July 1916. Over 300 of their number had died during the siege, Arab casualties are unknown. The surrender of the garrison had brought the Arab army five artillery pieces, as well as over 8,000 rifles and a large quantity of ammunition. In many ways the difficulties in Mecca prophesied later events in the revolt. In the months of warfare to come, Arab forces found on several occasions that they lacked the firepower to press home an attack.

At Ta'if, in the highlands to the south-east of Mecca, Sharif Hussein's son, the Emir Abdullah, had arrived with a small force of tribesmen near the town around 5 June 1916. The governor of the Hejaz, Ghalib Pasha, was then in Ta'if and Abdullah informed him that he was in the area to carry out a raid against another Arab tribe. During the days that followed, further Arab forces arrived to join Abdullah. By 10 June, he had a force of over 5,000 tribesmen.

Having cut the telegraph link to Mecca, Abdullah and his tribesmen went into action in the evening of 10 June attacking the north side of the town. The military commander at Ta'if, Ahmad Bey, had strengthened the town's defences in the weeks preceding the attack. Abdullah's tribesmen, who again lacked support weapons, could not press home their attack. Over the following days a number of other attacks failed and the situation descended into a siege. Occasional sorties by the Ottoman troops failed to drive off the Arab tribesmen. In mid-July help arrived for the Arabs in the form of the same Egyptian battery that had shelled the fortress at Mecca. Yet even with their help, the siege was not ended until 22 September when the garrison surrendered.

The outbreak of the revolt at Medina was less auspicious. Arab forces under the emirs Ali and Feisal had gathered in the vicinity of the town on 5 June. Having sent a formal notice to the Turkish military commander, Fakhri Pasha, that the Arabs were breaking off relations with the Ottoman Government, they began military operations and carried out attacks on the railway in order to disrupt communications. On 8 June, they attacked the railway station at Muhit, to the north of Medina, but were driven off by the garrison. Worse was to follow as Fakhri Pasha had emerged from Medina with a force of at least two brigades. He fell upon the Arab rear and then pursued them southwards. Ali and Feisal split their forces in the hope of dividing the pursuers. As he advanced southwards, Fakhri Pasha fortified and garrisoned towns along his route to facilitate future operations. At the outbreak of the revolt, Ottoman forces in Medina numbered around 12,000 men. As the city remained in Turkish hands, they could strengthen this force and begin a counterattack. There was no reason to believe at this time that the Arab Revolt would survive the year.

THE CAPTURE OF THE COASTAL TOWNS AND THE ARRIVAL OF AID FROM THE ALLIES

The Arab leaders had recognized that the capture of coastal port towns on the Red Sea would be crucial for the survival of their revolt. As the initial attacks were occurring at Mecca, Ta'if and Medina, other Arab forces were advancing to seize ports on the Red Sea coast.

The forces of Sharif Mushin Mansur forced the surrender of the Turkish garrison at Jiddah, aided by seaplane attacks from the Royal Navy carrier HMS *Ben-My-Chree*. In late July both Yanbu and Rabegh fell into Arab hands.

The initial force of Egyptian troops that facilitated the taking of Mecca and Ta'if had arrived at Jiddah in July. Also in July, the first contingent of 700 volunteers had arrived for the Arab Regular Army. Former POWs, and predominantly of Iraqi origin, they were commanded by Nuri as-Sa'id. They brought with them a battery of 4.5in. howitzers, four mountain guns, eight machine guns, explosives and 4,000 rifles.

The initial main base was at the port of Jiddah, which was placed under the command of Colonel Cyril Wilson. With the help of a small number of officers, including Lieutenant (later Major) H. Garland, the town was fortified. Garland would later take part in a series of attacks against the railway. By October, the British and French had established military missions to the Arab Army under colonels Wilson and Brémond respectively and they had representatives in the coastal towns, while the French also had military personnel, drawn from Muslim units, in Mecca. The Arab Regular Army was also being reinforced and, now under the command of Ali al-Masri, it provided much-needed support to the Arab irregular armies. Contingents of the Regular Army had been sent into the field and had already joined the irregular forces of the emirs Feisal and Ali in the hope of impeding Turkish countermoves. Despite these improvements to the Arab situation, the autumn

The house of the British mission at Wejh. One of the tribesmen in the foreground appears to be carrying an SMLE rifle. (Bailloud collection, SHD, Vincennes)

Turkish countermoves on Yanbu and Rabegh, 1 December 1916 to 18 January 1917

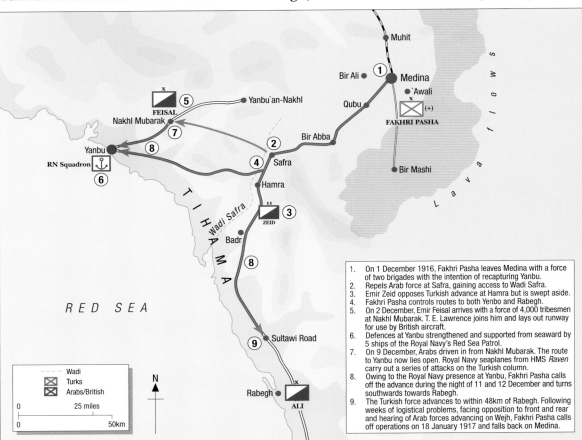

1. On 1 December 1916, Fakhri Pasha leaves Medina with a force of two brigades with the intention of recapturing Yanbu.
2. Repels Arab force at Safra, gaining access to Wadi Safra.
3. Emir Zeid opposes Turkish advance at Hamra but is swept aside.
4. Fakhri Pasha controls routes to both Yenbo and Rabegh.
5. On 2 December, Emir Feisal arrives with a force of 4,000 tribesmen at Nakhl Mubarak. T. E. Lawrence joins him and lays out runway for use by British aircraft.
6. Defences at Yanbu strengthened and supported from seaward by 5 ships of the Royal Navy's Red Sea Patrol.
7. On 9 December, Arabs driven in from Nakhl Mubarak. The route to Yanbu now lies open. Royal Navy seaplanes from HMS *Raven* carry out a series of attacks on the Turkish column.
8. Owing to the Royal Navy presence at Yanbu, Fakhri Pasha calls off the advance during the night of 11 and 12 December and turns southwards towards Rabegh.
9. The Turkish force advances to within 48km of Rabegh. Following weeks of logistical problems, facing opposition to front and rear and hearing of Arab forces advancing on Wejh, Fakhri Pasha calls off operations on 18 January 1917 and falls back on Medina.

months of 1916 were difficult for the forces of the Arab Revolt. The Turkish forces under Fakhri Pasha had swelled to include 12 battalions of infantry, plus various supporting units. He had continued to operate against Arab forces south of Medina and was determined that the Arab Revolt would end within the year.

It was in October 1916 that Lawrence joined the Arab Army in the field. He had been released by the Intelligence Department in Cairo and attached to the Arab Bureau. With Ronald Storrs, he was dispatched by ship to Jiddah to assess the situation in the Hejaz and also suggest further courses of action. An implicit part of his mission was to assess the various Hashemite leaders and determine which of these was most likely to prosecute the war effectively against the Turks. It is impossible in the space of this short study to describe fully the political machinations that followed. But it must be pointed out that Lawrence, despite his youth and lack of field experience, quickly summed up the qualities of the various Arab leaders. He dismissed the emirs Ali and Abdullah for various reasons. Perhaps in reality this was because they were less prone to foreign manipulation. He fixed his attention on the Emir Feisal, whom he recognized as being a charismatic leader and also as the leader who perhaps had the least to gain from the political dispensation as it then stood. On Lawrence's recommendation, Feisal would receive increasing amounts of support from Britain, in terms of both money and military

The ammunition dump and guard tent at Wejh. For the remainder of the campaign, both the British and the French military missions strove to keep the Arabs supplied with food, clothes, equipment and small arms. The provision of artillery was a much-debated issue. (Bailloud collection, SHD, Vincennes)

matériel. He would also be re-directed northwards to satisfy both his own kingly ambitions and British military purposes. Feisal was then encamped near Yanbu with around 9,000 men.

Lawrence returned to Cairo to report before setting out again for the Hejaz on 25 November. His arrival was timed to coincide with the most serious crisis yet faced by the Arab leaders. Having maintained contact with the Arab armies throughout October and November, Fakhri Pasha advanced out of Medina on 1 December 1916 with three full brigades with the intention of reinforcing his army in the field and retaking Yanbu. He immediately outflanked the tribesmen of the Bani Salem who were holding the Wadi Safra to the west of Medina. The Emir Zeid, Hussein's youngest son, rushed to Hamra to oppose the Turkish advance, only to be swatted aside. Feisal moved to Nakhl Mubarak to the east of Yanbu in the hope of diverting the main thrust of Fakhri Pasha's advance, and, although his force was attacked, there seemed to be no way of deflecting the Turkish commander from his intention. Here Lawrence found Feisal during the night of 3/4 December and they discussed their future plans.

In the action that followed, the Arabs were pushed back from Nakhl Mubarak and it seemed that Yanbu would be recaptured and that Feisal's army would be destroyed or scattered. At Yanbu itself, where the defence was under the command of Garland, some attempt was being made to put the town into order but there were only 1,500 Arab troops available. It was the arrival of five ships of the Royal Navy's Red Sea Patrol that threw the balance back in the Arabs' favour.

In the course of the whole campaign the Royal Navy often played a crucial role not only by supplying the Arab armies but also by covering the port towns in moments of crisis. In this case, five Royal Navy ships including HMS *Dufferin* and the *M.31*, a monitor capable of moving close inshore, had arrived to cover Yanbu with their guns and searchlights. The Royal Navy force also included the seaplane carrier HMS *Raven*, which dispatched seaplanes to attack the Turkish column. The failure of the Turkish force to press home an attack during the night of 11/12 December effectively ended their hopes of recapturing Yanbu. Lawrence later stated that it also ended their chances of regaining control in Arabia.

Intimidated by the presence of RN ships and RNAS planes, Fakhri Pasha then turned his intention southwards and he advanced within 50km of Rabegh before this advance stalled. While the forces of the emirs Ali and Zeid seemed too weak to stop the Turkish advance, once again Fakhri Pasha's force was subjected to air attack, this time from a flight of RFC planes now operating from Yanbu. The Royal Navy also moved ships to cover Rabegh and thereafter a series of further problems emerged for the Ottoman commander. He was facing logistical difficulties as his supply lines stretched back to Medina and were subject to attack from tribesmen. In the last weeks of 1916 the Turks found it difficult to maintain the momentum of their advance and in early 1917, Fakhri Pasha revived news that a Turkish column under Ashraf Bey had been captured near the oasis of Khaybar. This Turkish force had been overrun by a force led by the Emir Abdullah and it was found that they were escorting over £20,000 in gold coin. Furthermore, he was informed that a large Arab force was marching on Wejh, one of the last Ottoman-held ports on the Red Sea, while RFC planes were flying raids on Medina. On 18 January 1917, the Turkish offensive was called off and Fakhri Pasha marched his army back to Medina.

This was not, however, the end of Turkish countermoves south of Medina. In March 1917, Ottoman forces were joined by Ibn Rashid and his tribesmen and carried out a sweep to the west. There would also be further operations against the Arab armies later in the autumn of 1917. Ultimately, it could be argued that in failing to re-take Yanbu in December 1916, the Turks had lost the initiative in the campaign. They would find themselves confined to Medina for the remainder of the war. Equally the armies of the emirs Ali and Abdullah would remain in this southern part of the Hejaz for the rest of the war as they countered the Ottoman forces. The Arab advance on Wejh signalled the beginning of a new phase of the campaign that would eventually lead the Arab Northern Army to Damascus.

THE CAPTURE OF WEJH, DECEMBER–JANUARY 1917

In the middle of December 1916, the Emir Feisal decided to move his army northwards, away from Yanbu, in order to take the port of Wejh further up the coast. There were immediate military reasons for doing this. Wejh was one of the last major ports on the Red Sea coast still in Ottoman hands, and the last anywhere near Mecca and the other towns in Arab possession. Moving a large Arab force northwards would also force the Turks to react and thus take pressure off the Arab forces at Yanbu, Rabegh, Mecca and Ta'if. It was this threat of Arab attacks that had caused Fakhri Pasha's counteroffensive to stall. This Arab move northwards would also ultimately extend Fakhri Pasha's right flank all the way to Damascus, which was 1,300km away, and force the Turks to spread their troops thinly to protect the railway line.

The Emir Abdullah took his army to Wadi 'Ais and from there he could still cover Yanbu while being in a position to attack the railway. In the first days of the new year, Feisal led his army northwards from Nakhl Mubarak. His force included 1,200 tribesmen of the Agayl and also members of the Juhayna, the Harb and the Billi. Further tribesmen joined the army as they travelled and soon the force was over 8,000 strong. It was the largest Arab army in living memory.

As Auda ibn Hamad, sheikh of the Rifa'a, commented it was 'not an army, but a world which is moving on Wejh'. In cooperation with the Royal Navy, it was arranged that Wejh would be taken by simultaneous assaults from seaward and landward. The Royal Navy would support a landing in the port of Wejh, which would be carried out by Arab tribesmen. Feisal and Lawrence would press home an attack from the landward side. On the morning of 23 January 1917, a small flotilla of Royal Navy ships moved close inshore to Wejh. Commanded by Admiral Wemyss, they included HMS *Hardinge*, HMS *Fox* and HMS *Espiegle* and carried around 600 Arab volunteers. This small Arab force was commanded by Major Charles Vickerey, Captain N. N. E. Bray and sheikhs 'Amar and Salih from the Arab Army. The town was garrisoned by around 800 men of the Turkish 129th Infantry Battalion, supported by a camel corps of 500 Agayl.

Supported by naval gunfire and a naval landing party, the force attacked the town, fighting from street to street during the day. The promised attack by Feisal, Lawrence and their tribesmen from the landward side did not materialize. Sections of the town had still not fallen by sunset but the next morning it was found that the Turkish commander had evacuated the rest of the town. Only a small party of Turkish soldiers remained in the mosque and they soon surrendered. Feisal and Lawrence and the Arab Army did not arrive until 25 January. While recriminations flowed freely in the aftermath of this attack, it had secured its goal and the port of Wejh became a base for the build-up of the Arab Northern Army. It also became the main base for the next phase of the revolt, which saw a series of raids taking place against the Hejaz Railway.

THE RAILWAY CAMPAIGN, 1917

The capture of Wejh greatly facilitated Feisal and Lawrence's plans to mount a campaign against the Hejaz Railway. The philosophy behind these railway attacks was quite simple. The attacks were to be serious enough to prevent the Turkish garrison at Medina from being re-supplied properly. This in turn would prevent Fakhri Pasha from engaging in serious offensive operations. It would also force the Turkish garrison at Medina and further north at Ma'an to dissipate their forces in defending the railway.

This general plan would develop further. By March 1917, General Murray was planning to advance across Sinai. Lawrence was then informed that it was imperative that the Medina garrison be prevented from evacuating the city. The forces of Fakhri Pasha, numbering over 12,000 troops, could not be allowed to reach Palestine, or even Ma'an. The ultimate philosophy behind the railway campaign therefore was to incapacitate rather then destroy the Turkish army in the Hejaz. The large garrison at Medina almost became captives as they lacked the capacity to mount a major offensive operation while at the same time they could not evacuate along the railway in safety. In March 1917, Fakhri Pasha was ordered to leave Medina – orders that he successfully protested against.

It is impossible to cover this campaign in extensive detail here, but from early 1917 small parties of Arabs left Wejh to undertake attacks against the railway, commanded by officers such as Colonel Newcombe, Lieutenant (later Major) H. Garland and Lieutenant Hornby. Arab regular officers, such as Major al-Masri, also went on these railway raids. Their methods were simple and they concentrated on finding unguarded sections of line

ATTACKS ON THE HEJAZ RAILWAY, FEBRUARY 1917 (pp. 40–41)

While there had been a series of attacks on the Hejaz Railway in the preceding months, in February 1917 Lieutenant H. Garland **(1)** became the first Allied officer to successfully mine a moving locomotive **(2)**. To do so he used a mine with a contact detonating device that had been fashioned from an old Martini-Henry rifle. This type of device came to be known as a 'Garland mine' and it allowed sabotage teams to place mines that needed no telltale command cord to detonate them **(3)**. On several occasions mines were laid at night and the attacking forces could depart hours before a train was even due. Attacks on the railway would continue throughout the war and

T. E. Lawrence would later lead attacks on stations and bridges as well as on locomotives. Alongside attacks using explosives, later demolitions along the railway became more brazen and Arabs and Allied officers pulled up sections of rail, demolished bridges and destroyed water stations. Such attacks were later facilitated by covering parties that had Rolls-Royce armoured cars while, from 1917, sabotage parties were also aided by RFC/RAF aircraft. In turn, the Ottoman Army had to devote huge resources to maintaining and guarding the Hejaz Railway. It was vital for the survival of the Turkish garrisons in Arabia and would tie down Turkish divisions for the remainder of the war.

A Turkish supply train at the station at Kissir, south of Amman. The Hejaz Railway had been completed using German engineers and employed German locomotives and rolling stock. In theory it was a pilgrim railway linking Damascus to Medina, the railhead for the holy city of Mecca. In practice it was of major military importance for the Ottoman Army and became a target of Arab attacks. (IWM Q59650)

and destroying them with explosives. In some cases, if it was safe and time permitted, they would lever up sections of track by hand to conserve explosives. The parties were initially kept small in an effort to avoid detection and usually numbered two officers and perhaps a dozen tribesmen. These parties would later grow in size and in 1917 could vary between 40 to 200 men. During these larger raids, some men could be used to demolish sections of line while others provided support.

In February 1917, Lt. Garland succeeded in mining a moving locomotive using a contact mine that he had devised himself. This used the mechanism of an old Martini-Henry rifle as a trigger device. This type of contact mine came to be known as a 'Garland mine'. The ambitions of the demolition officers then extended to cover attacks on Turkish locomotives and rolling stock. Soon Col. Joyce, who had been placed in charge of logistical matters at Wejh, found himself deluged with demands for explosives, detonators, exploder boxes and also lengths of electrical cable. He later commented that 'all energies have to be concentrated on line smashing'.

Newcombe, Garland, Hornby and other officers developed methods for destroying the railway that reached exquisite proportions. While, initially, demolition parties had gone in for spectacular attacks that included trying to derail trains and setting off huge explosions on the line, they soon realized that they could employ other methods to perhaps greater effect. To create more disruption, by the summer of 1917, they focused their attention on damaging large sections of the line. They attacked curved sections at bends in the line, knowing that these rails would be harder to replace. They used 'tulip mines', which bent metal rails into fantastical tulip shapes, to damage long sections of the line. These methods forced Turkish repair parties to remove difficult, tangled sections of line before they could actually replace them and this doubled the time and manpower expended to repair the line.

Lawrence, who had been attached as a permanent liaison officer with Feisal's Army, also began to take part in these attacks. Instructed from Cairo to keep the Turkish Army in Medina, in March 1917 he travelled south to Wadi 'Ais to make contact with Abdullah and encourage him into greater efforts against the railway. It was during this expedition that he later claimed that he had executed one of his own party – a man known as 'Hamed the

Moor', who had murdered one of the Agayl. Having delivered his message to Abdullah, Lawrence then set out on a raid of his own, attacking the line between Aba al-Na'am and Istabl Antar.

This was the first time that Lawrence had actually seen the railway for himself and his party succeeded in mining the track north and south of the station at Jabal Unsayl and also in cutting the telegraph line. With Sharif Shakir he took part in an attack on the railway station and one of his mines partly derailed an approaching train. Although driven off by Turkish fire and disappointed with the result, Lawrence's raid had been a success. It would be the first of many raids.

Lawrence continued his raids throughout the early summer of 1917, attacking both the line and also station buildings at different locations. The other officers of the British mission were also keeping busy. The station at al 'Ula had been identified as a key target because of its plentiful supply of water. In June, Feisal, Newcombe, Joyce and Hornby took a party of Arab regular troops, tribesmen, Egyptian and Indian troops to attack the line both north and south of this important station. During the night of 6/7 July, Newcombe, Joyce and their party laid over 500 charges on railway sleepers to the south of al 'Ula and then detonated them at 2am. Hornby laid a further 300 charges to the north of al 'Ula. Similar attacks continued over the next few nights and on 11 July, RFC planes arrived to bomb al 'Ula by day. This was just one of many big raids but it demonstrates how the line could be cut and then kept closed for a number of days. For those involved, it was a deeply pleasing task. Colonel Joyce later wrote 'the noise of the dynamite going was something grand and it is always satisfactory finding one is breaking things'.

In the months that followed, the demolition parties damaged stations, water towers and especially bridges. Joyce later recalled how he and Lawrence demolished either end of a stone bridge but left the centre section tottering on the brink of collapse – delighting in the knowledge that the Turks would have to engage in a dangerous demolition before replacing the whole bridge.

Such activity was not confined to the Arab Northern Army. In February 1917, at the same time that Newcombe, Garland and Hornby were beginning their attacks, the French mission were also organizing attacks on the line

north of Medina. Capitaine Raho, formerly of the 2e Régiment de Spahis Algérien, carried out the first such attack when he set out in February with a small party of Bedu to mine the line. Further attacks were undertaken and Raho had increased the size of his force by August 1917 to 40 French troops and around 200 Bedu. In August he embarked on a major raid, attacking the line north of the station at Mudurij. Despite being under fire from the Turkish garrison, Raho and his men calmly went about their business of mining the line and succeeded in destroying five kilometres of track and four bridges. He returned to the Emir Abdullah's camp at Abu Markha on 30 August, having covered over 340km in nine days and without losing any men. For this action, Raho was promoted to be an officer of the Légion d'honneur and was also awarded the Military Cross by the British Government.

A Turkish repair gang working on a damaged section of the Hejaz line. It is believed that Lawrence, rather cheekily, took this photograph having caused the initial damage. The Ottoman Army expended large resources in keeping the line open during the war. (IWM Q60166).

The railway raids played a vital part in the revolt in 1917 and were a huge boost to Arab and Allied morale. Such attacks became a feature of the campaign throughout 1917 and 1918. Lawrence had begun the war as a military amateur but he realized that a new fighting doctrine was emerging out of the Arab Revolt. He later summed up the philosophy behind the raids: 'Most wars were wars of contact, both forces striving into touch to avoid tactical surprise. Ours should be a war of detachment. We were to contain the enemy by the silent threat of a vast unknown desert, not disclosing ourselves till we attacked. The attack might be nominal, not directed against him, but against his stuff; so it would not seek either his strength or his weakness, but his most accessible material.'

AQABA, JULY 1917

While these raids were being carried out, the Arab Northern Army remained based at Wejh. During this period, the composition of the irregular contingent of the army began to change. Some of the more southern tribesmen began to leave and head southwards to return to their homelands. The men of the Juhayna for instance began to leave for their homeland in the Wadi Yanbu. At the same time, tribesmen began to arrive from the north, men whose homelands were in Syria or the Syrian marches. They included tribesmen from the Howeitat, the Shararat, the Bani 'Atiya and the Rwalla.

These northern tribesmen urged Feisal to move the revolt northwards through Palestine and onward to Syria. Their leaders included Auda abu Tayi, whose Howeitat had their homeland to the east of Ma'an. They also included the Syrians Nasib al-Bakri and Zaki Drubi, who promised a widespread revolt in their homeland if the Arab Northern Army took the campaign there. In many ways, they were preaching to the converted. Feisal had long been convinced that the Hejaz could not survive as an independent state without some connection with the more fertile regions of Palestine and Syria. From a personal point of view, he knew he must also look towards Palestine and Syria to satisfy his kingly ambitions. Furthermore, the Arab leaders had known the details of the Sykes–Picot Agreement since May 1917. It was now rumoured that over 60,000 French troops were going to be landed in Syria. Feisal knew that he must act if he was to have any hope of securing any chance of ruling these lands. If an Arab army was in possession of Palestine and Syria, then surely they would have considerable moral and political leverage in any post-war conference.

While Lawrence felt that a Syrian uprising at this time would be premature, he also recognized the need to regain the initiative in the campaign. He opposed the idea of French control of Syria and had also been shocked at the revelations of the Sykes–Picot Agreement. His attention focused on the port town of Aqaba, the last Red Sea port in Ottoman control. If it could be seized for Feisal's Army, it would change the whole direction of the campaign and its location would facilitate operations into Palestine and Syria. If the Arab Northern Army was based there it would also be nearer to the main Allied army and could assist in future operations.

Lawrence and Auda abu Tayi. In July 1917, they led an Arab force in an epic route march which ended with the capture of Aqaba. The capture of this crucial port was one of the major coups of the war and Aqaba then served as the main base for further operations to the north. (IWM Q60702)

The Royal Navy had shelled Aqaba from the seaward side, but the coastal defences were felt to be too strong to allow a landing. Lawrence now came up with the plan of taking it from the landward side. Auda and also the Syrian leaders supported him in this and he convinced Feisal of the viability of the plan. It is now obvious that he was disingenuous with his fellow British officers at Wejh, including Col. Joyce, who was in command of Operation *Hedgehog*, as the British mission to the Arab Northern Army had been christened. As Lawrence presented it, he was planning a long-range raid to the vicinity of Ma'an. It was to be timed to coincide with a major raid that was being carried out by Col. Newcombe in the direction of al 'Ula.

On 9 May 1917, he left Wejh with a small party. He was accompanied by some of the best leaders of the Arab Revolt, all of whom had displayed highly developed tactical abilities in the past. Sharif Nasir was in tactical command and the party also included Auda and Za'al Abu Tayi, Nasib al-Bakri, Zaki Drubi and Mohammed adh-Dhaylan. As the Arab tribesmen would not fight outside of their tribal homelands, they took only 17 Agayl fighters with them, who were commanded by their chief Ibn Dgaythir. They carried over £20,000 in gold coin with them with which they intended to recruit tribesmen, predominantly from the Howeitat, in the vicinity of Aqaba.

Arab tribesmen in Wadi Ithm on 5 July 1917, before the attack on Aqaba. Their approach from the landward side took the outlying Turkish garrisons totally by surprise. (IWM Q59207)

The Arab capture of Aqaba, July 1917

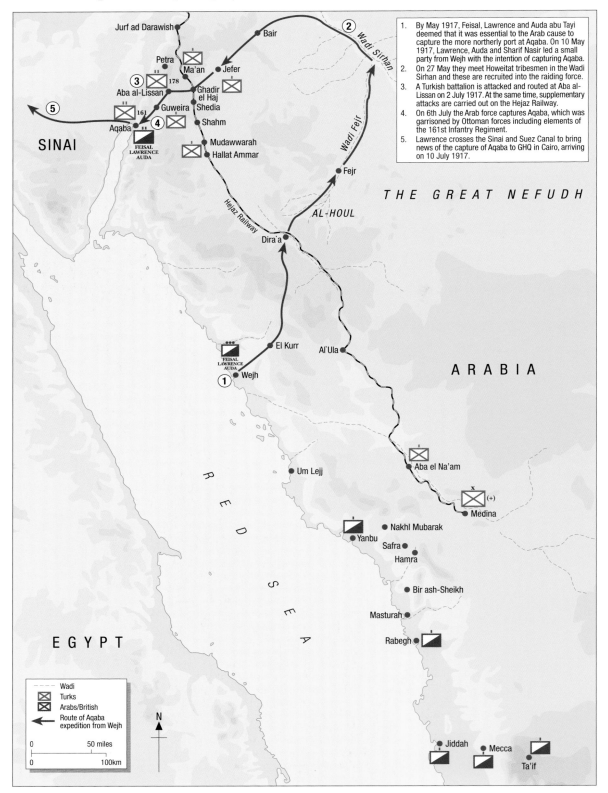

1. By May 1917, Feisal, Lawrence and Auda abu Tayi deemed that it was essential to the Arab cause to capture the more northerly port at Aqaba. On 10 May 1917, Lawrence, Auda and Sharif Nasir led a small party from Wejh with the intention of capturing Aqaba.
2. On 27 May they meet Howeitat tribesmen in the Wadi Sirhan and these are recruited into the raiding force.
3. A Turkish battalion is attacked and routed at Aba al-Lissan on 2 July 1917. At the same time, supplementary attacks are carried out on the Hejaz Railway.
4. On 6th July the Arab force captures Aqaba, which was garrisoned by Ottoman forces including elements of the 161st Infantry Regiment.
5. Lawrence crosses the Sinai and Suez Canal to bring news of the capture of Aqaba to GHQ in Cairo, arriving on 10 July 1917.

Legend:
- - - - Wadi
Turks
Arabs/British
Route of Aqaba expedition from Wejh

0   50 miles
0   100km

N

SINAI

EGYPT

ARABIA

THE GREAT NEFUDH

AL-HOUL

R E D   S E A

Jurf ad Darawish
Bair
Petra
Ma'an
Jefer
Aba al-Lissan
178
Ghadir el Haj
Guweira
Shedia
Aqaba
Shahm
FEISAL LAWRENCE AUDA
161
Mudawwarah
Hallat Ammar
Wadi Sirhan
Wadi Fejr
Fejr
Dira'a
Hejaz Railway
El Kurr
Al`Ula
FEISAL LAWRENCE AUDA
Wejh
Um Lejj
Aba el Na'am
Medina
Nakhl Mubarak
Yanbu
Safra
Hamra
Bir ash-Sheikh
Masturah
Rabegh
Jiddah
Mecca
Ta'if

In his biography of T. E. Lawrence, Michael Asher has described the Aqaba expedition as 'one of the most daring raids ever attempted in the annals of war'. They planned to approach Aqaba by carrying out a huge sweep to the north-east. This would necessitate covering over 1,000km of the worst terrain in Arabia including a section of desert known as 'al-Houl', 'the Terror'. The small party would travel down the Wadi Sirhan, a major corridor of communication, and there they hoped to recruit Howeitat tribesmen. They would then descend south-westwards down the Wadi Ithm to attack Aqaba from the land. As they drew further northwards, Lawrence planned to launch attacks on the railway, to distract the Turks from the mission's true objective.

This was to be an expedition of epic proportions. Lawrence himself later wrote of the harshness of the desert. 'Bedouin ways were hard even for those brought up to them, and for strangers terrible: a death in life.' The reality of these words was brought home to all of the party as, for weeks, they trekked through some of the worst desert terrain in Arabia. On crossing the railway line on 19 May, they dynamited a section of it and also cut the telegraph lines. On one occasion, Lawrence returned alone to look for one of his servants, Gasim, who had fallen from his camel and been left behind. It was an incredibly selfless act for any man to undertake in such a hostile and dangerous location.

Having endured hunger, thirst and braved raiding parties, the party began to encounter friendly tribesmen around the end of May. Some of these were recruited for the Aqaba attack. Leaving the main force in Wadi Sirhan, Lawrence struck off to head even further northwards. In a round trip of over 800km he headed to the outskirts of Damascus, where he met with Arab leaders and implored them not to rise up too soon against their Ottoman overlords. En route, he demolished a bridge near Ras Baalbek with the help of Metawila tribesmen. This attack led to the fear of a general uprising among the Metawila, which led the Turks to move six battalions out of the front line. Lawrence had also carried out a major reconnaissance of the region and this would facilitate the later Allied advance into Palestine and Syria. He arrived back at Nabk in the Wadi Sirhan on 17 June.

Perhaps one of the most evocative images to emerge from World War I. This photograph was taken by Lawrence and shows the Arab Army dashing into Aqaba. Beyond the Sharifian standard-bearer, other horse-mounted tribesmen can be seen charging. (IWM Q59193)

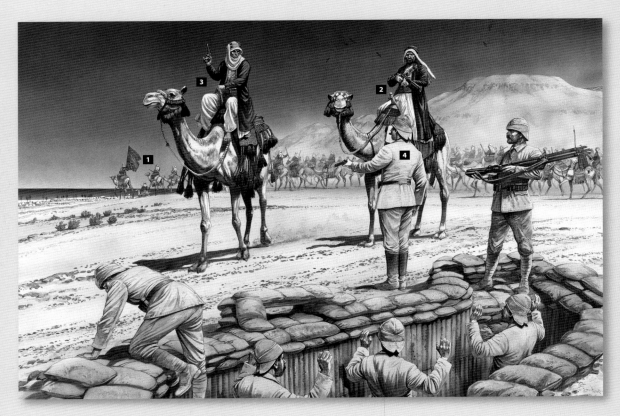

THE FALL OF AQABA, JULY 1917 (pp. 50–51)

In the summer of 1917, T. E. Lawrence and the Arab leaders recognized the importance of seizing the port of Aqaba in order to secure a port and base on the northern Red Sea coast that could in turn facilitate further campaigns into Palestine and Syria. Accompanied by a party of tribesmen (1) and Auda abu Tayi (2) , the hereditary war chief of the warlike Howeitat tribe, Lawrence (3) led a small force on an epic two-month march through the desert. After a clash with a Turkish battalion at Abu al-Lissan, the Arab force took the surrender of some of the outlying garrisons and finally took Aqaba on 6 July 1917. The taking of Aqaba represented a huge turning point in the orientation of the campaign and thereafter the Arab Northern Army could use it as a base for later campaigns in support of General Allenby's push into Palestine in 1917 and 1918. Depicted here is the surrender of the final Turkish garrison

at Khadra, outside Aqaba (4). The port town then became the major base of the Arab Northern Army, which was commanded by the Emir Feisal. In the months that followed, the Arab Northern Army was reinforced and resupplied by sea and in later campaigns it included an armoured car detachment and mobile artillery battery while the RFC/RAF provided further support. In the campaigns of 1918 this Arab force represented a considerable threat to the Turkish left flank while attacks on the railway continued along the length of the Hejaz Railway, further draining Turkish resources. All this was made possible by Lawrence's daring expedition to Aqaba in 1917. The Aqaba raid became a model for later long-range desert operations and during World War II inspired the leaders of units such as the LRDG and the SAS to carry out similar raids during the North Africa campaign.

The port of Aqaba showing the seaward side. (IWM Q59548)

In his absence the Arab leaders had recruited the force that would ultimately take Aqaba. It consisted of over 500 men of the Howeitat, 150 Rwalla and Shararat tribesmen and 35 men of the Kawakiba. They set out on their final march towards Aqaba, finding that the Turks had destroyed many of the wells along their route. On 30 June, a detached party of Howeitat from the main force took the Ottoman fort Fuweilah, killing members of the garrison almost to a man in retaliation for a Turkish massacre of some of the local population. This fort was retaken by a battalion from the Turkish 178th Regiment, which had arrived from Ma'an to support the local garrisons. While a series of attacks were carried out against the railway, news reached Lawrence and the Arab leaders that this Turkish battalion was encamped around the well at Aba al-Lissan. It was the last major Turkish unit between the Arab force and Aqaba.

As the morning of 2 July dawned, Lawrence and the Arab tribesmen were positioned in the hills overlooking Aba al-Lissan and the Turkish battalion encamped there. The attack began with a prolonged period of inconclusive sniping and skirmishing. As the day grew hotter, the attack stalled and by afternoon, many of the tribesmen were shading from the sun, as was Lawrence himself. It was an exchange between Auda abu Tayi that regained the momentum of the attack. Lawrence's calculated insult that the tribesmen 'shoot a lot and hit a little' incited Auda's anger and spurred him to organize a charge of 50 or so tribesmen. These riders swept through the Turkish force and ended their resistance. Lawrence and Nasir then led 400 camel-riders in a final attack to cut off the enemy's pursuit, in which Lawrence managed to shoot his own camel in the head on account of his excitement. For the cost of two Arab tribesmen who were killed, the Turkish battalion had been destroyed, suffering around 300 fatal casualties while the commanding officer and around 160 men were taken prisoner. The Arab force had also captured a mountain gun.

In the days that followed, the outlying Turkish garrisons at Guweira, Kathira and Hadra surrendered; one of the captured Turkish officers sending letters into the besieged troops telling them that they would be treated fairly. As the Arab force approached Aqaba, they found further outposts abandoned. On the evening of 5 July, they reached the final Turkish post at

HMS *Humber* moored in the port at Aqaba. The Royal Navy provided crucial support for the Arab bases along the Red Sea coast and the guns and searchlights of their ships covered the Arab forces on shore. (IWM Q59064)

Khadra and there was some sniping that evening and the next morning. There were also attempts to secure the surrender of the garrison. By this time, the Arab force had swelled to over 1,000 men as further tribesmen from the Howeitat and the Haywat had joined them. The Turkish commander at Khadra, realizing that no support could make it to him from Ma'an, agreed to surrender on the morning of 6 July. By chance, a Royal Navy gunboat, the *Slieve Foy*, had arrived off the port and had subjected it to further shelling. When Lawrence took the surrender of the Turkish troops at Khadra on 6 July, the tribesmen then dashed into Aqaba to find that the rest of the garrison had abandoned the town. The final assault took place without a shot being fired.

It was perhaps one of the greatest coups of the war. An Arab irregular force had not only defeated a regular Turkish battalion at Aba al-Lissan but had taken a major port on the Red Sea. The seizure of Aqaba also changed the orientation of the Arab Revolt totally and made operations into Palestine a serious possibility. Lawrence had to get this information to Cairo as soon as possible and set out on 7 July to cross Sinai to get to Suez and from there to GHQ in Cairo. He later claimed to have crossed the desert in 49 hours, which has since been shown to be impossible. However, when he did reach Cairo on 10 July, he found that a new GOC had been appointed to the Egyptian Expeditionary Force. General Murray's failure in two attacks on Gaza had led to his removal. His replacement by General Sir Edmund Allenby coincided with the Arab capture of Aqaba.

Still dressed in Arab robes, Lawrence was granted an interview with Allenby and informed him of Arab plans to rebel in Palestine and Syria. While Allenby's real impression of Lawrence is sometimes hard to gauge, it seems apparent that he immediately recognized the strategic advantages he now possessed because of the Arab seizure of Aqaba. He promised to send whatever help he could. In many ways, this meeting was as crucial for the future of the revolt as the capture of the port had been.

JULY–NOVEMBER 1917

In the weeks that followed, supplies poured into Aqaba while the Royal Navy maintained a presence in the harbour to protect the port. Feisal's army was moved from Wejh to Aqaba, the regulars being moved by ship while the irregular tribal force made the journey by camel. Lawrence, who had been promoted to major, requested that he be placed in command of *Hedgehog* but this was refused. Colonel Joyce would remain in command at Aqaba.

Despite the generally positive trend, there was also a series of internal problems. Intelligence indicated that the Turks were making serious attempts to buy the loyalties of Auda abu Tayi and although he did not defect, such overtures were made to other Arab leaders, including Feisal, later in the campaign.

Equally, the effects of the Sykes–Picot revelations were still being felt and it could be argued that the Arab-British relationship had been fatally damaged and would never be the same again. There were tensions within the Arab camp itself and Sharif Hussein increasingly tried to exercise control over Feisal. Despite the Arab success in taking Aqaba, an inertia fell over the Arab Northern Army and the momentum went out of the campaign.

The move to Aqaba had also created an immediate military difficulty. The port was within range of Ottoman planes at Ma'an and was subjected to bombing raids on an almost daily basis. The flight of RFC planes that had been based at Yanbu was rushed up the coast to counter this threat and they soon were buzzing over Ma'an, which would become the focus of considerable attention over the following months.

Raids upon the railway continued and were carried out by Joyce, Newcombe, Lawrence and various British and Arab officers. As further operations into Palestine were now planned, other activities were also planned in preparation for later campaigns. Long-range reconnaissance expeditions were undertaken to find overland routes into Palestine. There were also expeditions in search of sources of water. As the RFC was playing an increasingly important role in the campaign, Lawrence and his companions

A destroyed station building on the Hejaz Railway at Wadi Rutm. (Courtesy of the Great Arab Revolt Project)

RIGHT TOP
Wadi Rum photographed by a member of an armoured-car patrol. A hostile environment, this was one of the seasonal resting places of the Howeitat tribe and a favourite location of Lawrence, a place he returned to 'clear his senses'. (IWM Q59363)

RIGHT BOTTOM
Left to right, Captain Wood, Captain Thorne and Lawrence during an expedition. Wood is checking an SMLE rifle while Lawrence appears to be loading a Colt .45 automatic pistol. (IWM Q60099).

were constantly on the lookout for viable landing strips. In August 1917, Lawrence travelled into the Sinai to find and set out a rudimentary airstrip. This was then stocked with fuel and bombs and could be used by planes flying from Egypt on missions to bomb Ma'an and other Turkish outposts.

During the night of 17 September, Lawrence led a raid against the station at Mudawwarah, which lay almost directly due east from Aqaba. His intention was to destroy the well there and success would have meant that there was no large source of water for the railway for over 240km. He was accompanied by tribesmen and two British Army NCOs, Sergeant Yells and Corporal Brook, who were experts in the use of the Lewis gun and Stokes mortar respectively. The Turkish garrison of over 300 men was more than twice the size of Lawrence's force and a direct assault was ruled out. He decided to lay a large mine on a nearby bridge, which he detonated as a train of ten wagons, pulled by two locomotives, was passing over it. The result

The abandoned Crusader castle at Azrak, near Amman. During November 1917, Lawrence based his force at this castle, before and after the raid to the Yarmuk Valley. (IWM Q60022)

was a spectacular train wreck and Lawrence carried out further demolitions on one of the damaged locomotives to put it beyond repair. All the while, he and the Arabs were covered by Yells and Brook firing their Lewis gun and Stokes mortar at the approaching Turks. He also later noted that the wrecked train had been carrying both women and sick. It is certain that, despite his outward bravado, such events took a heavy toll on Lawrence. As he wrote to a friend around the same time, 'nerves going and temper wearing thin'.

After further railway raids that he undertook with Capitaine Pisani of the French mission, Lawrence went to Cairo for a meeting with General Allenby. They discussed possible operations that could be mounted in support of wider British plans. A Syrian uprising was ruled out and Allenby asked Lawrence to mount a raid into the Yarmuk Valley in order to cut the branch line of the Damascus–Medina line that ran through it. This was a vital artery between Palestine and Syria, and the raid was to coincide with Allenby's planned offensive on the Beersheba–Gaza line, which was timed for the end of October. If Lawrence could cut a major bridge across the valley it would prevent Turkish supplies and reinforcements reaching the front line. It was also hoped, if the offensive was successful, the Ottoman Army would not be able to retreat out of Syria if the line was cut. Allenby asked him to do this during the night of 5 November, or during the three following nights. Such a deep penetration mission into Turkish-held territory was viewed by some of Lawrence's fellow officers as a suicide mission.

Lawrence left Aqaba on 24 October 1917 with a raiding party of tribesmen. His party also included machine-gunners from the Indian Army and Lieutenant Wood, an expert in demolition from the Royal Engineers, who would supervise the demolition of the Yarmuk Valley Bridge. This was

Arab tribesmen and officers of the Arab Regular Army in a Talbot car at Wadi Ithm in March 1918. The Emir Feisal sits in the front right seat while Auda abu Tayi is behind the driver wearing a white head cloth. (IWM Q60048)

a crucial mission but one that was to lurch from one crisis to the next. Among the group was Abd al-Qadir (or Abd el-Kader) who lived among Algerian exiles in the Yarmuk. He was descended from the Abd el-Kader (1808–83) who had led North African tribesmen in their resistance to the French in the late 19th century. Colonel Brémond of the French mission had warned Lawrence that al-Qadir was a Turkish spy, a warning that Lawrence chose to ignore. During the night of 4 November, al-Qadir and his men disappeared and it seemed that the mission had been compromised. It also proved difficult to recruit the tribesmen of the Serahiyyin, who feared local reprisals.

Lawrence pressed on nevertheless. Having secured the support of some of the local Serahiyyin, his small force set out to blow the bridge at Tel ash-Shehab during the night of 7 November. The attack descended into a shambles. During their approach march, a local farmer fired on them, taking them for raiders. It began to drizzle rain and, as Lawrence crept towards the bridge with the explosives, a tribesman dropped his rifle, the noise alerting the Turkish guards. As the Turkish soldiers fired into the darkness, Lawrence's party scattered. The tribesmen carrying the explosives abandoned this hazardous cargo fearing that they would be blown to smithereens if a bullet should hit one of their boxes. When the party finally re-assembled, Lawrence found that they no longer had enough explosives to destroy any of the bridges over the Yarmuk. The mission was aborted. As Lawrence retreated, he could hear the British artillery in the distance.

During their retreat, Lawrence and his men mined the line at Minifir, north of Deraa, destroying two culverts and a train being pulled by two locomotives. Owing to the fact that he had not enough cable, he had to detonate the mine too close to the track. He later wrote 'when I peered through the dust and the steam of the explosion, the whole boiler of the first engine seemed missing. Just in front of me was the scalded and smoking upper half of a man.'

It turned out that the train was that of General Mehmed Cemal Pasha ('Mersinli'), commander of the Ottoman VIII Corps. The party returned to its base at the castle at Azrak, east of Amman, on 12 November. The next days in Lawrence's life remain surrounded in mystery. It is known that he remained at Azrak for some days and during this time met with Syrian

The cooperation of the RFC and later the RAF greatly facilitated the Arab Revolt. Here an RAF officer (perhaps Lieutenant Murphy) demonstrates the armament of his Bristol Fighter to an Arab tribesman in 1918. In the final phases of the revolt, the RAF air support was crucial. (IWM Q58702)

leaders, including Talal al-Haraydhin of Tafas. According to his later account in *Seven Pillars of Wisdom*, he travelled to Deraa to reconnoitre the town and arrived there around 20 November. There he claims he was captured by the Turks and subjected to a rape. This whole episode remains the focus of debate. Some Lawrence scholars have found inconsistencies in the recorded dates in his field journals. While the modern consensus on this episode seems to tend towards disbelief, it will remain a topic of contention for everyone interested in the Lawrence story.

What is certain is that he returned to Aqaba on 25 November. In his absence, the Arab Northern Army had not been idle. In early October, Col. Joyce and Maulud al-Mukhlis had led a party of over 300 men of the Arab Regular Army on a raid to the west of Ma'an. During this expedition, they captured the old Crusader fort at Shawbek, which was being used as a Turkish garrison. They remained for just a short time, realizing that to stay would invite retaliation against the local population. Joyce and al-Mukhlis realized that this was a subtext to all the plans to incite revolt in Syria. The Syrian tribesmen would have to have Allied help to hand before they could rise in revolt. Otherwise, they would suffer from Turkish reprisals.

On 21 October, a large Turkish force attacked the Arab Regular Army outpost at Wadi Musa near Petra. Commanded by al-Mukhlis this small force held its ground and drove off the Turkish attackers with heavy loss. The Arab Regular Army had come of age and was ready to play an important role in the forthcoming campaigns.

The Arab Army at Aqaba had also been significantly reinforced. Capitaine Pisani now commanded a battery of French mountain artillery. Armoured cars had previously worked with the Arabs in the fighting around Yanbu and a squadron of Rolls-Royce armoured cars had been attached permanently to Feisal's Army in November 1917. A squadron of Talbot cars, some of which carried 10-pdr guns, and some Ford light cars supplemented these. This increased both the mobility and firepower of the Arab Army and throughout December, Joyce and Lawrence tested these cars over the rough ground of Wadi Ithm and also along the new roads that were being built around the port.

The crashed BE2 of Lieutenant Junor, which was forced down while supporting a raid on Yarmuk in September 1918. On being shot down, Junor then attached himself to Lawrence's force and helped crew an armoured car. (IWM Q60019)

Despite these improvements this was not a positive time for the Arab Revolt. On taking power in Russia, the Bolsheviks had leaked the full details of the Sykes–Picot Agreement. The negative fallout from this was exacerbated when details of Arthur Balfour's support of a Jewish homeland in Palestine became known. Balfour, who was then the Foreign Secretary of the British Government, had written to Lord Rothschild in early November 1917 stating that the Government supported Jewish claims for a homeland in Palestine.

This letter was published in *The Times* on 7 November. It could not have come at a worse time for the Arab Revolt. Already filled with doubts about their alliance with the British, the Arab leaders now looked to the future with some scepticism. The Ottoman leaders in turn wasted no time and Cemal Pasha (commander of Fourth Army and Governor of Syria) made conciliatory speeches in Damascus and made contact with the Arab leaders, announcing an amnesty for past transgressions. Furthermore, in November a train was ambushed north of al 'Ula and was found to be carrying over £24,000 in gold. It seems certain that this money was to be used to try to buy back the Arabs.

The Arab Revolt had reached yet another critical juncture. Owing to the considerable diplomatic skills of Lawrence and other officers, the Arab leaders were kept on side. The Allied cause was much helped by the capture of Jerusalem on 9 December 1917. To even the most sceptical of the Arab leaders, it was obvious that the Ottoman star was in the descendant. The Arabs also felt that they had a powerful ally in America. In his famous 'Fourteen Points' speech, delivered in a joint session meeting on 8 January 1918, President Woodrow Wilson declared that the 'other nationalities which are now under Turkish rule should be assured an undoubted security of life and an absolutely unmolested opportunity of autonomous development'. Perhaps the conditions of the final settlement of the former Ottoman territories could be re-negotiated at the end of the war.

THE FINAL CAMPAIGN, PALESTINE AND SYRIA, DECEMBER 1917 TO OCTOBER 1918

While November 1917 had been a time of disappointment and also acrimony between the Arab leaders and the officers of *Hedgehog*, the year ended on a more positive note. Military successes in December 1917 and January 1918 suggested that perhaps a new and decisive phase of the campaign was about to begin.

Since the arrival of the Rolls-Royce armoured cars and the Talbot car battery, Lawrence, Joyce and other officers had been experimenting in their use. They tried them over different types of terrain and this allowed Lawrence to indulge in his love for speed. Sam Rolls, one of the armoured-car drivers later wrote of how Lawrence urged him onwards, until the speedometer hit 113kph.

In preparation for further expeditions, depots were laid down to the east of Aqaba. Joyce, Lawrence and other officers realized that this comparatively small group of cars actually represented quite a strong mobile force and they decided to use them in a long-range raid against the important railway station at Mudawwarah.

They set out on 26 December 1917 and, on reaching the railway line, engaged in a reconnaissance of the station and the surrounding area. They found that they were impregnable to Turkish rifle and machine-gun fire and Lawrence would later describe this as 'fighting de luxe'. While they decided that the station was too strong for them, they did manage to destroy some railway wagons and also shelled the nearby station at Tell Shahm, using the 10-pdrs mounted on the Talbot cars.

The irregulars of the Arab Northern Army were also far from idle. A force of over 1,100 tribesmen and Arab regulars, commanded by Sharif Nasir and Nuri as-Sa'id, opened the new year by seizing Abu al-Lissan, the site of an important well between Aqaba and Ma'an that had been retaken by the Turks. They then continued to carry out a raid on the line north of Ma'an, capturing the station at Jurf ad Darawish and over 200 Turkish soldiers.

A Turkish tent ring being excavated by members of the Great Arab Revolt Project in Wadi Rutm. (Courtesy of the Great Arab Revolt Project)

THE BATTLE OF TAFILA, 25 JANUARY 1918

The Turkish attempt to recapture the village with a composite brigade that had advanced southwards from Kerak.

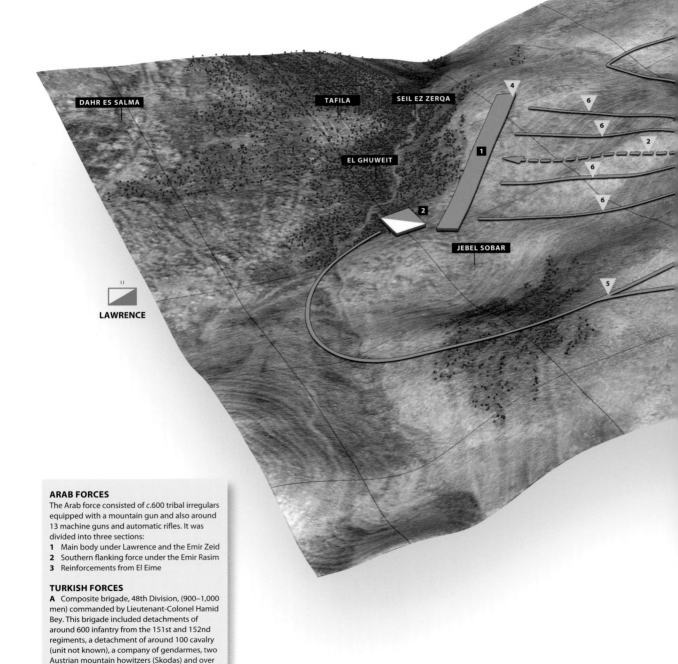

DAHR ES SALMA

TAFILA

SEIL EZ ZERQA

EL GHUWEIT

JEBEL SOBAR

LAWRENCE

ARAB FORCES
The Arab force consisted of *c.*600 tribal irregulars equipped with a mountain gun and also around 13 machine guns and automatic rifles. It was divided into three sections:
1 Main body under Lawrence and the Emir Zeid
2 Southern flanking force under the Emir Rasim
3 Reinforcements from El Eime

TURKISH FORCES
A Composite brigade, 48th Division, (900–1,000 men) commanded by Lieutenant-Colonel Hamid Bey. This brigade included detachments of around 600 infantry from the 151st and 152nd regiments, a detachment of around 100 cavalry (unit not known), a company of gendarmes, two Austrian mountain howitzers (Skodas) and over 20 machine guns and automatic rifles.

Note: Gridlines are shown at intervals of 500 mtrs/547 yds

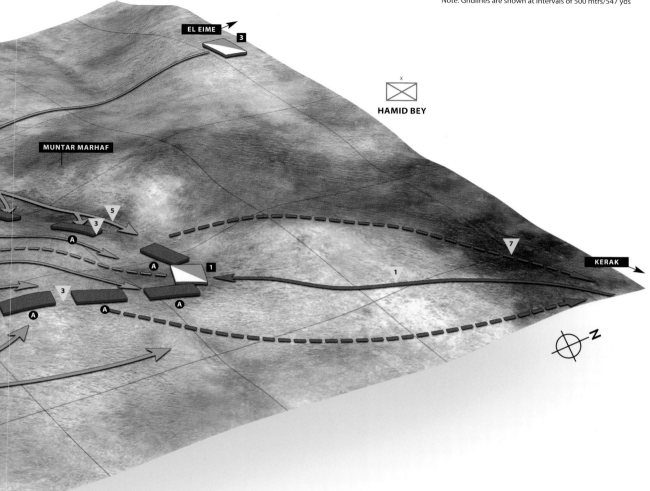

EL EIME **3**

HAMID BEY

MUNTAR MARHAF

KERAK

▼ EVENTS

1 Around midday: early in the afternoon of the 25 January 1918, Arab scouts report advance of Turkish cavalry on the road from Kerak. These opposed at ridgeline, 2,750m to the east of Tafila, where the road runs between the two lines of ridges.

2 1230hrs: the original Arab detachment was reinforced but on reconnoitring the Arab position, Lawrence decided to draw back all his forces to the westwards to re-form along ridgeline to the east of Tafila and the wadi El Ghuweit.

3 1300–14.00hrs: the Turkish commander occupied the ridgeline where the Arabs had originally opposed his advance. The Turkish positions formed an inverted triangle, facing westwards. Interspersed in his infantry units, the Turkish commander placed over 20 machine guns and automatic rifles. On his left flank he positioned his two mountain howitzers.

4 1400hrs: a spirited exchange of fire developed. Lawrence deployed his machine guns and automatic rifles in the centre of his position and also a mountain gun. At the same time, around 100 men from El Eime moved southwards to reinforce the Arabs.

5 1600hrs: The Emir Rasim took 80 men and began a sweep to the south with the intention of enveloping the Turkish left flank. Simultaneously the party from El Eime attacked the Turkish right flank. Both forces succeeded in reaching the rear of the Turkish positions before putting in their attack, using wadis and ridgelines for cover and advancing to within 180m.

6 1620hrs: Lawrence thinned his main line to provide support to the flanking parties but on seeing confusion in the Turkish lines, led his main force in a frontal attack.

7 1630hrs: the Turkish line collapsed. Those who could retreated and fled back along the Kerak road or to the east. Many were cut down on the way or captured. The Turkish commander later died of wounds. Around 300 were killed and 200 taken prisoner. The Arabs also captured both mountain howitzers, 16 machine guns and around 200 horses. The Turkish wounded were left to lie out overnight and died of exposure (it snowed that night). Around 20–30 Arabs were killed and 90 wounded.

Ford cars, Talbot cars and Rolls-Royce armoured cars at Abu al-Lissan in 1918. The firepower of these mobile units aided both tribesmen and the Arab Regular Army in their attacks. Some of the Talbot cars were mounted with 10-pdr guns while the Rolls-Royce cars carried Vickers machine guns. The numerous spare tyres carried here speak volumes about the terrain. Such units pioneered methods of desert travel that were later used in World War II. (IWM Q59529)

During its return journey, Sharif Nasir's force captured the town of Tafila (also Et Tafilah). This small town, around 70km north of Ma'an, was set in the fertile uplands of the Wadi Araba. It was in the middle of an important grain-producing region and was a vital source of food for the Ottoman Army. It was obvious that the Turks would try to recapture it and the Arabs prepared for a defence of the town. The Emir Zeid, the younger brother of Feisal, was sent to take charge of operations and Lawrence arranged for an urgent shipment of £30,000 in gold to be sent from Palestine to Tafila in order to raise levies of tribesmen, which could then be used to support Allenby's planned advance into Palestine.

Around 22/23 January, a composite brigade formed by units of the Turkish 48th Division left Kerak, to the north of Tafila, under the command of Lieutenant-Colonel Hamid Fakhri Bey. The size of this force remains unclear, with some sources stating that it numbered around 600 while others state 1,000. As it included a cavalry force, infantry from the 151st and 152nd regiments and also had two mountain guns and over 20 machine guns of different types, it may be safe to assume that it numbered around 900–1,000 men. Turkish sources number the infantry contingent alone as being 600 men, which would not seem unreasonable. This force reached the vicinity of Tafila in the evening of 25 January and there was some initial skirmishing to the north of the town. The next morning the Turkish force made a determined effort to retake the town and put in their main assault around midday. Nasir, Lawrence and the other Arab leaders had only around 600 men, four mountain guns and around a dozen light machine guns to counter this superior Turkish force.

The battle of Tafila has been largely forgotten in the history of the revolt but it can be viewed as one of the major achievements of the Arab Army.

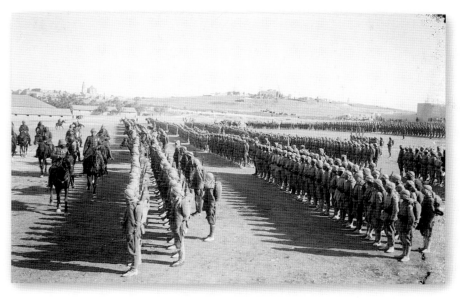

They initially opposed the Turkish force to the north of the town but were driven back to occupy a ridgeline facing the Turkish troops. Lawrence later referred to this as the 'Reserve Plateau' or 'Reserve Ridge'. The Turks in turn occupied two ridgelines to the north of the town and a brisk firefight developed that lasted for most of the afternoon. In this exchange, the Arabs made the better use of their artillery. Towards 4pm, further Arab tribesmen arrived from the north and they put in an attack on the Turkish right flank. The original force on the 'Reserve Ridge' then put in a simultaneous frontal assault and an attack on the Turkish left flank. In the face of this three-pronged attack, the Turkish force faltered and broke. The remnants of the Turkish brigade retreated northwards towards Kerak. Around 200 had been killed while over 250 were captured. The prisoners included Hamid Fakhri Bey, who had been mortally wounded while trying to rally his troops. He died later that evening.

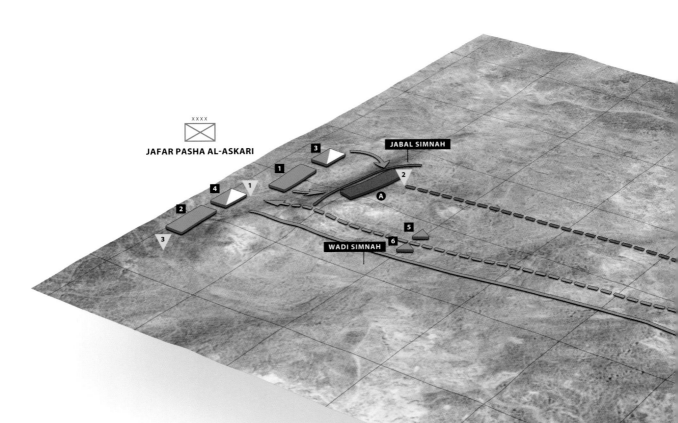

XXXX

JAFAR PASHA AL-ASKARI

JABAL SIMNAH

WADI SIMNAH

EVENTS

1 The Arab Regular Army reaches the vicinity of Ma'an around 12 April 1918.

2 At dawn on 13 April, an attack by the Arab 1st Division seizes the Jabal Simnah.

3 The following days are spent consolidating and planning – an assault on the town is not at first planned. There are also references to the taking other high ground to the west of Ma'an but it is unclear where this was.

4 In the morning of 16 April, the 2nd Division puts in a main assault with the objective of taking Ma'an Station. This attack stalls in the evening, within 200m of Turkish wire in some places.

5 On the evening of 17 April, the attack is renewed with the aid of Howeitat tribesmen and breaks through the Turkish defenses. It reached the station building before being repelled.

6 Arab force retreats back to starting positions. Much criticism follows concerning their lack of artillery support, especially with regard to Capitaine Pisani who had run out of ammunition.

7 Surrender negotiations begun but when the garrison at Ma'an is reinforced by 3,000 troops from Amman, these are called off. The Ma'an garrison holds out until September 1918.

ARAB FORCES
Arab Regular Army
1 1st Division (800 men), Brigadier-General Amin al-Asil.
2 2nd Division (800 men), Lieutenant-Colonel Majid Hasun

Tribal contingents
3 Wadi Musa tribesmen with the 1st Division
4 Howeitat tribesmen under Auda abu Tayi and Hejazi tribesmen commanded by Sharif Fahd with the 2nd Division

Artillery
5 Two guns under Arab command
6 Two guns under Capitaine Pisani.

TURKISH FORCES
A 1st Kuvve-i Mürettebe – an all-arms unit, its main infantry units were supplied by the 79th, 138th and 161st infantry regiments. It also included cavalry, MG detachments, artillery and a gendarmerie detachment.

THE ARAB REGULAR ARMY ATTACK ON MA'AN, 13–17 APRIL 1918

This unsuccessful attack developed out a plan to raid north and south of Ma'an to cut the railway line.

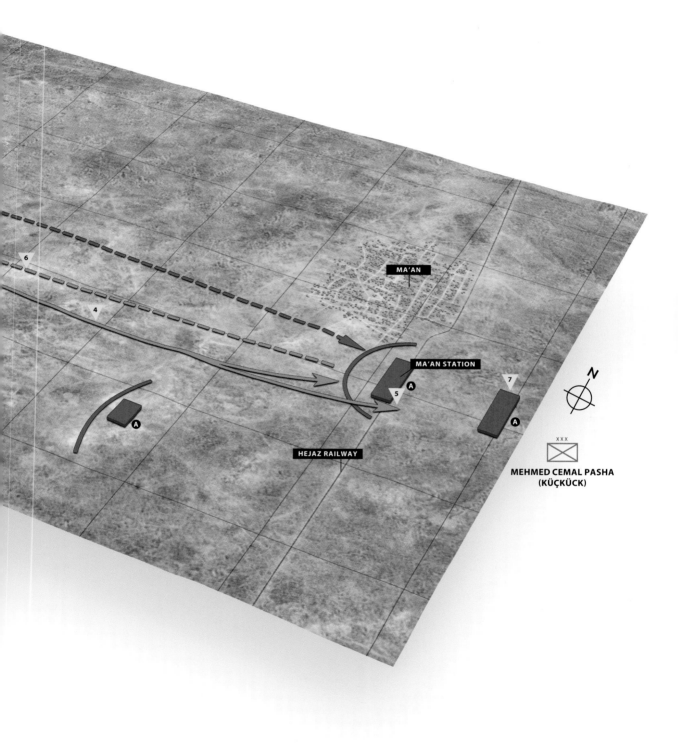

Note: Gridlines are shown at intervals of 1000 mtrs/1093 yds

6

4

MA'AN

MA'AN STATION

5

A

7

A

N

HEJAZ RAILWAY

XXX

MEHMED CEMAL PASHA
(KÜÇKÜCK)

67

Lawrence was typically disingenuous in his later comments on the action, saying that he had sent in a semi-satirical report to GHQ, portraying the battle as though he had taken part with a copy of Clausewitz's *On War* in his hand. Nevertheless, he was awarded a DSO. Soon afterwards tribesmen destroyed the fleet of small Turkish boats that ferried supplies across the Dead Sea. It was a remarkable success by an irregular force against a superior force of regular soldiers commanded by an experienced officer.

The euphoria over Tafila was short lived. Finding that Zeid had already spent the £30,000 that was intended for the new campaign, Lawrence departed for a meeting with Allenby, totally disillusioned with the revolt. While GHQ was prepared to overlook the loss of these funds, the plans formulated by Allenby and Lawrence for combined efforts had limited success. Further Arab operations were planned to support Allenby's advance on Amman. It was decided that a major attack would be launched against Ma'an on the Turkish left while the main British effort was concentrated on Amman. Ultimately both components of this combined operation failed. While the British offensive took Es-Salt and advanced towards Amman, a major Turkish counterattack was launched on 2 April, which drove them back.

To the south, Jafar Pasha al-Askari led the Sharifian Regular Army of around 4,000 men in an offensive in the vicinity of Ma'an. The original plan had been to cut the line to the north and south of this major action. But senior officers within the Arab Army, including Nuri as-Sa'id were confident that they could take the town of Ma'an in a concerted campaign. An initial attack on the station complex at Jardunah was a success despite the fact that the position was heavily entrenched. When the attack had stalled, Jafar Pasha al-Askari unleashed his violent temper and a torrent of abuse that spurred his men on. The Arab regulars stormed the trenches and took the surrender of around 200 Turkish soldiers.

TOP
A forgotten meeting in the desert, somewhere in Syria in 1918. Capitaine Pisani of the French mission (back to camera) encounters Arab tribesmen. (SHD, Vincennes)

CENTRE
Capitaine Pisani talking with Arab tribesmen, Syria 1918. Pisani had some experience of desert warfare having served in North Africa before the war. Here he wears a khaki tunic and a cheich scarf. (SHD, Vincennes)

BOTTOM
Arab tribesmen, photographed in Syria in 1918. (SHD, Vincennes)

THE ATTACK ON MUDAWWARAH STATION, AUGUST 1918 (pp. 70–71)

In the early hours of 8 August 1918, a force of 314 men drawn from the yeomanry companies of the Imperial Camel Corps emerged from the desert to attack the strategically important railway station at Mudawwarah (1). This station had been the focus of previous attacks but on this occasion it was taken and held. The success of the ICC attack indicated the final phase of this campaign had begun. In an attack directed by Major Robin Buxton (2), the ICC put in a conventional assault on the Turkish positions and bombing parties were supported by Lewis gun teams (3) in order to clear a series of Turkish redoubts. Later in the day, a final Turkish redoubt to the north of the station was bombed by the RAF until it too surrendered (4). While such

attacks are usually associated with the Arab forces, by 1918 they were being supported in the field by British and Commonwealth troops and these included elements from the Indian Army. The yeomanry companies proved themselves to be especially suitable for retraining as camel-mounted infantry and as such carried out long-range operations of which the attack on Mudawwarah Station is perhaps the best known. The camel corps of this war were part of a long tradition within the British army of training soldiers to serve as camel-mounted infantry – a tradition that stretched back to the Egypt and Sudan campaigns of the 19th century. The remains of the station at Mudawwarah still stand to this day.

The attack on Ma'an proved more problematic as a network of trenches and redoubts surrounded it. On 13 April, Maulud al-Mukhlis led an attack on the outlying redoubt at the Jebal Simnah to the west of Ma'an and was wounded in the process. The attack on the main garrison, numbering over 4,000 men, stalled amid fierce fighting on 16 April. While some of the Arab troops had penetrated the Turkish wire and advanced as far as the station on 17 April, they could not consolidate their gains and had to fall back on the Jebal Simnah.

The Ma'an situation settled down to a siege that would last until the end of the war. Further raids by tribesmen and also the armoured cars and the camel corps cut the line to the north and south. The Ma'an garrison was now be cut off in the same way as the Medina garrison was further south. They were, however, strongly entrenched and able to withstand further Arab attacks. Jafar Pasha's request to be allowed to use mustard gas to break the siege was later refused.

Attempts to negotiate a surrender of the garrison also failed when they were reinforced by 3,000 troops from Amman. To compound these setbacks, Allenby's second advance on Amman was also turned back in late April. These reverses could not have come at a worse time for the whole campaign in the Middle East. Owing to the German Spring Offensives of March 1918 on the Western Front, Allenby's Army was stripped of divisions in April and May.

This restricted Allenby in terms of offensive action and the combined Turkish and German armies that faced him could consolidate their defences. They could even engage in offensive action and Liman von Sanders launched a surprise offensive in mid-July, which was eventually beaten back.

For Lawrence and the leaders of the Arab Revolt, they redoubled their efforts against the railway. Operation *Hedgehog* was now commanded by Colonel Alan Dawney, and with Lawrence and other British officers he

Ancient funeral towers, near Palmyra in Syria, 1918. The photographs and maps of Allied officers greatly added to the historical and geographical knowledge of Arabia. Before the outbreak of the revolt, little was known of the interior and the Syrian territories, and the Ottoman authorities did not encourage map-making westerners. (SHD, Vincennes)

Arab advance on Damascus and Aleppo, 16 September to 28 October 1918

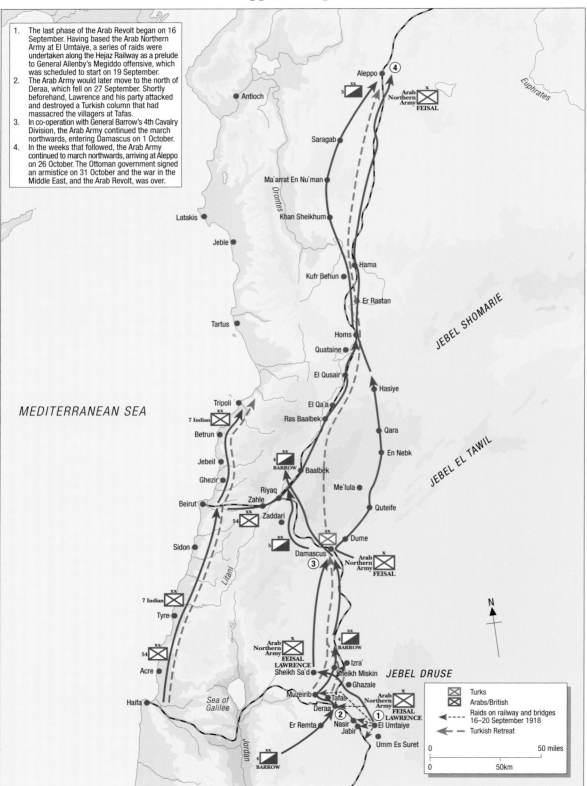

1. The last phase of the Arab Revolt began on 16 September. Having based the Arab Northern Army at El Umtaiye, a series of raids were undertaken along the Hejaz Railway as a prelude to General Allenby's Megiddo offensive, which was scheduled to start on 19 September.
2. The Arab Army would later move to the north of Deraa, which fell on 27 September. Shortly beforehand, Lawrence and his party attacked and destroyed a Turkish column that had massacred the villagers at Tafas.
3. In co-operation with General Barrow's 4th Cavalry Division, the Arab Army continued the march northwards, entering Damascus on 1 October.
4. In the weeks that followed, the Arab Army continued to march northwards, arriving at Aleppo on 26 October. The Ottoman government signed an armistice on 31 October and the war in the Middle East, and the Arab Revolt, was over.

Antioch

Aleppo ④

5 XX

Arab Northern Army
FEISAL X

Saragab

Ma`arrat En Nu`man

Latakis

Khan Sheikhum

Jeble

Orontes

Hama

Kufr Behun

Er Rastan

JEBEL SHOMARIE

Tartus

Homs
Quataine

El Qusair

Hasiye

MEDITERRANEAN SEA

Tripoli

7 Indian XX

Betrun

El Qa`a
Ras Baalbek

Qara

En Nebk

JEBEL EL TAWIL

Jebeil

Ghezir

4 BARROW XX
Baalbek

Me`lula

Beirut
Zahle
Riyaq

54 XX Zaddari

Quteife

Sidon

5 XX

Damascus
③

XX Dume

Arab Northern Army
FEISAL X

Litani

7 Indian XX

N

Tyre

54 XX

Acre

Arab Northern Army
FEISAL
LAWRENCE X

4 BARROW XX

Izra`
Sheikh Miskin

JEBEL DRUSE

Haifa

Sea of Galilee

Ghazale

Muzeirib
Tafas

Arab Northern Army
FEISAL
LAWRENCE X

Sheikh Sa`d

Deraa

Er Remta
Nasir
Jabir ①
El Umtaiye ②

Jordan

Umm Es Suret

BARROW XX

	Turks
XX	Arabs/British

Raids on railway and bridges 16–20 September 1918
Turkish Retreat

0 _____ 50 miles
0 _____ 50km

A splendid study of a Turkish officer with an Arab soldier of the Ottoman Army. From the Red Crescent insignia on the saddle, it would appear that this is a medical officer of the Ottoman Army. (Courtesy of the Library of Congress)

launched a series of major raids using tribal forces, the armoured cars, air support and a contingent from the Imperial Camel Corps. These attacks were far too numerous to detail here but they took place throughout the summer of 1918. In May 1918 alone, 25 bridges were demolished along the course of the railway.

In one of the most spectacular attacks, on 8 August 1918, Major Robin Buxton and his contingent of the Imperial Camel Corps captured the station at Mudawwarah. Mudawwarah was heavily defended and when the ICC had cleared all but one of the Turkish redoubts, RAF planes that were in support bombed the final position and forced its surrender. It is an indication of the level to which the desert forces had evolved by this stage of the war.

The final and decisive phase of the Arab Revolt was timed to coincide with Allenby's Megiddo Offensive of late September 1918. Having engaged in a plan of misdirection to confuse the enemy regarding his true intentions, Allenby planned to break through on a narrow front at Megiddo. His intention was then to use the Desert Mounted Corps to exploit the break-through and capture strategic towns and passes. The use of air power would be vital and, in Allenby's best-case scenario, crucial enemy units such as the Turkish XXII Corps would be cut off and effectively destroyed. British forces would follow a coastal and also an upland route and converge on Damascus. (See Bryan Perrett, Campaign 61: *Megiddo 1918* Osprey Publishing Ltd, Oxford, 1999.)

The Arab Northern Army played a crucial part in this plan. Feisal was to assemble the Arab Northern Army to the east of the River Jordan. When the main offensive began, this would tie down Turkish forces and also make the Turkish commanders nervous about the integrity of their eastern flank. In the weeks preceding the offensive, Lawrence and the other Arab leaders embarked on a recruiting tour and also organized a huge supply train using over 1,500 camels supplied by Allenby. At the beginning of September 1918, the Arab Northern Army began to assemble for the final campaign. Its main striking force contained around 450 Arab regulars and also a tribal contingent made up of men from the Howeitat, the Rwalla, the Bani Sakhr, Agyal and also Druses and villagers of the Hauran. Their tribal leaders

The railway yard at Damascus in September 1918. This yard was a terminus of the Hejaz Railway and had been fired by Turkish troops before they retreated. (IWM Q12371)

included Auda abu Tayi, Mohammed adh-Dhaylan, Nuri ash-Sha'alan and Talal al-Haraydhin.

Attached to this force there was also a party of camel-mounted Gurkhas, Egyptian Camel Corps and Capitaine Pisani and his Algerian gunners. The armoured-car squadron would also accompany them and during the course of operations Bristol Fighters of the RAF and, on one occasion, a Handley-Page bomber would support them. In the middle of September this small army of just over 1,000 men assembled at El Untaiye, to the south-east of Deraa. Feisal would later take this army slightly further south to Umm Es Suret to avoid being bombed by planes from Deraa.

Allenby had set 19 September for the beginning of the Megiddo offensive and, in the days before this, the Arab Army attacked the railway line to the north and south of Deraa. Effectively cut off, the Turkish garrison made huge efforts to repair this line. Bridges were destroyed, six kilometres of line were demolished and the line north of Mafraq station was also cut. Deraa, an important station on the line to Damascus, was isolated before the offensive began. Despite the pressure that the Turks were under, Lawrence and his force did not have it all their own way. They were driven away from the line by Turkish camel corps and also strafed on several occasions by both Turkish and German aircraft.

The progress of the main offensive was good and, as the Turks reeled backwards, the forces facing the Arab army began to lose their cohesion. It was the beginning of the end. On the morning of 27 September, the Arab force was encamped near the village of Tafas when it received news that two Turkish columns were converging on the area. One was of 6,000 out of Deraa while the other of 2,000 was coming from Mezerib. It was agreed that the second smaller column would be attacked as it passed the village.

The sequence of the events that followed is still hotly debated. It is certain that the Turkish soldiers had massacred the villagers of Tafas in reprisal. It has also been established that Talal al-Haraydhin, whose village this was, died in an attack on the Turkish column. Supported by Pisani's artillery, the rest of the Arabs then put in an attack on the retreating Turks. Included among the Turks were also some German and Austrian troops who put up a fierce resistance. Lawrence later wrote that he issued a 'no prisoners' order at the beginning of the attack and those who tried to surrender were shot or cut down on the spot. The real controversy surrounds the issue of those who succeeded in surrendering, who numbered around 250 and included Germans and Austrians. After the war Lawrence confided in a letter to his brother that he ordered them to be machine-gunned. It is still unclear if this actually happened and, if it did, if he had sanctioned it.

It has been suggested that the rape he suffered at Deraa in 1917 had brutalized Lawrence and that this excuses his actions at Tafas. Whatever the truth he described the event in horrific detail in his memoir, *Seven pillars of Wisdom*: 'In a madness born of the horror of Tafas we killed and killed, even blowing in the heads of the fallen and of the animals; as though their death and running blood could slake our agony.'

A visibly exhausted Lawrence on the balcony of a hotel in Damascus after the capture of the city. In the weeks that followed, he witnessed the disappointment of the Arab leaders as they realized that they would not govern the liberated territories. (IWM Q73534)

The Strategic Situation in the Hejaz, 1919

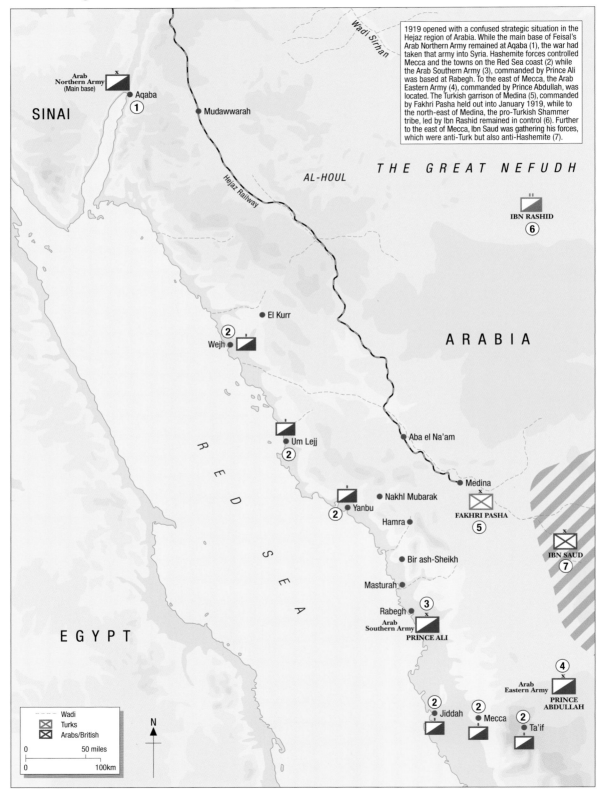

1919 opened with a confused strategic situation in the Hejaz region of Arabia. While the main base of Feisal's Arab Northern Army remained at Aqaba (1), the war had taken that army into Syria. Hashemite forces controlled Mecca and the towns on the Red Sea coast (2) while the Arab Southern Army (3), commanded by Prince Ali was based at Rabegh. To the east of Mecca, the Arab Eastern Army (4), commanded by Prince Abdullah, was located. The Turkish garrison of Medina (5), commanded by Fakhri Pasha held out into January 1919, while to the north-east of Medina, the pro-Turkish Shammer tribe, led by Ibn Rashid remained in control (6). Further to the east of Mecca, Ibn Saud was gathering his forces, which were anti-Turk but also anti-Hashemite (7).

SINAI

Arab Northern Army (Main base) ✕ ①

Aqaba

Mudawwarah

Hejaz Railway

AL-HOUL

THE GREAT NEFUDH

IBN RASHID ⑥

ARABIA

El Kurr

Wejh ②

Um Lejj ②

Aba el Na'am

Nakhl Mubarak

Yanbu ②

Medina

FAKHRI PASHA ⑤

Hamra

Bir ash-Sheikh

IBN SAUD ⑦

Masturah

RED SEA

Rabegh ③

Arab Southern Army ✕ PRINCE ALI

④

Arab Eastern Army ✕ PRINCE ABDULLAH

EGYPT

Jiddah ②

Mecca ②

Ta'if ②

Wadi Sirhan

Wadi
Turks ✕
Arabs/British ✕

N

0   50 miles
0   100km

The Turkish resistance was reaching its death agonies. Now totally isolated, the garrison of 4,500 men at Ma'an evacuated the town and began a long march to the north. Constantly harassed by tribesmen they surrendered to British forces in Transjordan on 28 September. On the same day, the Arab Army and the leading elements of General Barrow's 4th Cavalry Division reached Deraa. On their arrival, Barrow's men found Arab tribesmen slaughtering wounded Turks on a hospital train in the station. The British troops restored some kind of order but it was a grim epilogue to the events at Tafas.

There was now no real organized resistance between Deraa and Damascus. Turkish soldiers were surrendering in their thousands. The Arab Army swept on to Damascus, reaching that ancient city on 1 October along with elements of the 5th Cavalry Division and the Australian Mounted Division. Lawrence had sped northwards in a Rolls-Royce tender that he had christened 'Blue Mist'. Any jubilation was short lived. At a tense meeting in the Victoria Hotel on 3 October Allenby informed Feisal of the French claims to Syria and was astonished to find that Lawrence had not explained the details to him. While Feisal could govern Syria it would be under the guidance of the French. It seemed that the Arabs had shaken off their Ottoman overlords only to find them replaced with the French. The meeting ended inconclusively and boded ill for the future.

The pursuit of the Turks continued to Aleppo, which fell to Arab troops on 26 October. When Arab and British troops seized Muslimiya Junction on 29 October, the Allies effectively controlled the Turkish rail link to Mesopotamia. The Ottoman Empire was granted an armistice on 31 October. The Arab Revolt was at an end. Promoted to full colonel, Lawrence returned to England. Feisal and his followers faced an uncertain future. As James Barr pointed out in his recent study of the revolt, it was the success of the Arab Revolt that made the bad faith of the Allied leaders all the more apparent.

THE LEGACY OF
THE ARAB REVOLT

THE HEJAZ

On 25 May 1919, Capitaine Raho of the French mission was killed in action in the Taraba region of the Hejaz while serving with the Arab Eastern Army of the Emir Abdullah. His military career, which stretched back to the 1890s, came to a sudden and violent end in a forgotten corner of Arabia. Both Abdullah and Sharif Hussein later sent telegrams of condolence to Raho's family in Algeria and to the French Government. The action in which Raho was killed occurred long after the October 1918 armistice with Turkey and the end of the European war in November. Later official reports stated that he had been killed in an action with 'rebels from the east'. Who were these 'rebels' – Turks, Shammer tribesmen, the forces of Ibn Saud?

In many ways Raho's death confirmed the fact that military conflict still continued in the Hejaz, while it also prophesied the political turmoil that was to follow. From a military perspective, the situation at the beginning of 1919 was deeply unsatisfactory. Despite the success of Feisal's Army to the north, there had been no similar decisive campaign in the Hejaz. The Turkish garrison at Medina still held out after the armistice had been signed with

Arab tribesmen pass a group of Turkish prisoners after the capture of Damascus in 1918. (IWM Q12307)

Turkey. They had been cut off and besieged for several months but their commander, Fakhri Pasha, was determined to hold out. There had been plans to attack the city using the Arab Southern and Eastern armies and French forces but intelligence reports indicated that Fakhri Pasha intended to make a fight of it. He had almost 10,000 effectives and was well entrenched. It was not military action that forced the surrender of Medina, and Fakhri Pasha agreed to hand over the city only after a delegation came from Constantinople and convinced him to accept the armistice and its ramifications. He surrendered at Bir Darwish on 9 January 1919 along with 456 officers and 9,364 men.

The pro-Ottoman followers of Ibn Rashid, mostly from the Shammer tribe, still remained, however. Although less dominant since the defeat of their

The Emir Feisal with a group of his supporters at the Paris Peace Conference in January 1919. Lawrence is immediately behind him to the right, dressed in the uniform of an officer of the regular Sharifian Army. Directly behind Feisal is Capitaine Pisani, formerly the commander of the French contingent of the Arab Northern Army. Second from left is Nuri as-Sa'id, later premier of Iraq. In the rear of the group to the right is a member of Feisal's bodyguard. (IWM Q55581)

Ottoman masters, Ibn Rashid still maintained an army until he too was curbed in 1919, this time by the forces of Abdul Aziz Ibn Saud. In the years that immediately followed, it was the forces of Ibn Saud that emerged as the dominant force in the Hejaz. He had been supported and supplied by the British during the war and, in 1917, Harry St John Philby had been sent to make contact with Ibn Saud and sound out his intentions. For Philby, Ibn Saud seemed to be the leader most capable of uniting and ruling Arabia and, although vehemently opposed by Lawrence, it was Philby's view that eventually held sway with Government leaders in Britain. The Hashemites themselves were divided and could not resist the force of emerging Saudi power in Arabia. Despite the wartime assurances of the Allied governments, the Hashemites were left to fend for themselves in the face of increasing Saudi opposition.

In October 1924, Hussein abdicated in favour of his eldest son the Emir Ali, who was then proclaimed as emir of Mecca and king of the Hejaz. Yet the Hashemites were increasingly isolated in Arabia and, in December 1925, Ibn Saud finally unseated them in Arabia, taking control of the Hejaz and the holy cities of Mecca and Medina. The Hejaz therefore became part of the new kingdom of Saudi Arabia. Both Hussein and Ali went into exile. Hussein died in Amman in 1931 while Ali died in Iraq in 1935.

SYRIA

If it can be argued that the Allied powers declined to become actively involved in the confrontation between the Hashemites and Saudis in the Hejaz, it can be seen that they took a very active part in allocation of former Ottoman territory in other areas. Nowhere was this truer than Syria.

The Emir Feisal had led his army in the final campaign of the war in the hope of becoming king of Syria. He was bluntly told that this was not to be the case as early as October 1918. The Syrian territories fell within the French remit, as agreed under the terms of the Sykes–Picot Agreement. It was obvious that these allocations would now be debated in post-war conferences, but the French established Général Henri Gouraud as the French High Commissioner of Syria and Lebanon in 1919 while the finer details were being hammered out.

The Emir Abdullah, Winston Churchill and Sir Herbert Samuel, photographed during Churchill's official visit to Jerusalem in 1921. Abdullah would become king of Transjordan in 1923. (Courtesy of the Library of Congress)

The ultimate fate of the former Ottoman territories was decided in a series of conferences from 1919. Feisal attended the Paris Peace Conference of January 1919 with a delegation that included both Lawrence and Capitaine Pisani, but could not gain recognition as king of Syria. Two further conferences followed – the Conference of London (February 1920) and the San Remo Conference (April 1920), which were specifically aimed at deciding the fate of the former Ottoman territories. The decisions of the Allied powers were then agreed in treaties with Turkey.

Realizing that his claims would not be recognized, Feisal had continued to gather support in Syria. He was proclaimed as king by the Syrian national congress in March 1920. This was followed by a French military intervention that defeated Syrian forces at the battle of Maysalun on 23 July 1920. The battle at Maysalun, which is about 20km west of Damascus, was a largely one-sided affair. The 9,000-strong French force had the benefit of both tanks and aircraft and easily defeated the Syrian Army of around 3,000 men. Syrian dead numbered over 400 while the French lost 42. As a result of this defeat, Feisal was expelled from Syria. The French mandate to govern the Lebanon and the smaller states that make up modern-day Syria (Aleppo, Damascus, etc.) was confirmed by the League of Nations.

IRAQ

At the end of the war, the former Ottoman territory of Mesopotamia was in British control. This was renamed as the new state of Iraq. In 1920 a revolutionary war broke out against the new British administration after Britain had been granted the territory under their mandate.

The Iraqi war was the main focus of the Cairo Conference of 1921. At this conference Winston Churchill, who was then colonial secretary, assembled a panel of 40 experts or, as he nicknamed them, the 'forty thieves'. They included Lawrence, Gertrude Bell and also Jafar al-Askari, who was then Minister for War in Iraq. One of the outcomes of the Cairo Conference was the conclusion of an Anglo-Iraqi Treaty, which ended the war. It also saw the installation of Feisal as king of Iraq. This form of government would continue until the Baathist revolution of 1958.

For Feisal, it had been a long and difficult journey from the Hejaz to Iraq, via Palestine and Syria. The new state of Iraq would continue to be troubled by political upheavals throughout his reign. It is interesting to note that many

Général Henri Gouraud (saluting left-handed), French High Commissioner to Syria and commander-in-chief of the French Army of the Levant, arriving at Beirut in November 1919. Gouraud, who had lost his right arm in the Gallipoli campaign, would retain this appointment until 1923. (SHD, Vincennes)

of the leading figures of the revolt remained loyal to Feisal and had later careers in Iraq. Colonel Joyce, who had commanded *Hedgehog*, later helped organize and train the new Iraqi Army. Jafar al-Askari, former C-in-C of the Arab Regular Army, served several terms as both Minister for War and Prime Minister of Iraq. Nuri as-Sa'id, who had served as Jafar's chief of staff, also later served as Iraqi Prime Minister, holding that office no less than 14 times. Both Jafar al-Askari and Nuri as-Sa'id were later assassinated, in 1936 and 1958 respectively, which is testimony to the volatility of the internal politics of Iraq. King Feisal died in 1933 at the comparatively young age of 48.

PALESTINE AND JORDAN

Under the terms of the Sykes–Picot Agreement, the British area of control also included Palestine and Jordan, or Transjordan as it then was. In 1921 this mandate was confirmed by the League of Nations and in May 1923, the Emir Abdullah was recognized by the British as the king of Transjordan.

Abdullah had not only commanded the Arab Eastern Army during the revolt, but he had also acted as his father's Foreign Minister. When Feisal's Syrian forces had been defeated at Maysalun in 1920, he had begun to move an Arab Army towards Syria in his support. Following negotiations with Winston Churchill, Abdullah had called off further military action. While Abdullah's kingly ambitions had initially focused on the Hejaz and the Yemen, he now established a Hashemite kingdom in Transjordan. It was here that his father lived out his life in exile. On 20 July 1951, King Abdullah was assassinated by a Palestinian gunman while attending Friday prayers at the Al Aqsa Mosque in Jerusalem. He was succeeded by his grandson, King Hussein of Jordan (d. 1999), who later became one of the most influential figures in Middle Eastern affairs.

The post-war settlement in Palestine has proved to be the most problematic. It was governed by Britain under the terms of the British mandate and became the focus of a new phase of Jewish settlement in the

The emerging power in Saudi Arabia – the crown prince of Saudi Arabia, the Emir Feisal ibn Saud (standing fourth from left) on a shooting holiday in Co. Wexford in Ireland in 1919. This group of Saudi royals was accompanied to Ireland by Harry St John Philby (standing left) who emerged as one of the main brokers of the post-war Arabian settlement. During this visit, the party stayed at the shooting lodge of a local solicitor, Mr F. M. O'Connor. (Courtesy of the F. M. O'Connor collection)

decades that followed. This process was in keeping with assurances made by Britain from the Balfour Declaration onwards. By 1935, over 60,000 Jewish settlers had settled In Palestine. The subsequent tensions that developed between the Jewish and Palestinian communities destabilized the region and this remains the case up to today. It could be argued that the Israeli, Palestinian and international communities are still dealing with the results of the implementation of the various Allied mandates during the 1920s.

For the people of Arabia and the Syrian provinces, the implosion of Ottoman power following the war had profound effects. Few who became involved in the revolt could have imagined that the final dispensation would turn out as it did. The Middle Eastern region had been changed entirely, but for many their hopes for Arab government were quashed as various territories were doled out to be ruled under the terms of the Allied mandates. It was a far cry from the aspirations of the Arab leaders of 1916, be they Hashemite or Saudi supporters. The decades following the war have seen huge changes in the political demography of Arabia, Palestine, Lebanon and Syria but the traces of the wartime political manoeuvrings of the Allied powers can still be recognized.

The Arab Revolt also had profound effects on 20th-century military doctrine. Many of the methods used during the war were to be revisited during World War II, especially during the desert campaigns. The desert campaign had highlighted the weaknesses of the Ottoman position and illustrated how isolated desert garrisons were vulnerable to attacks on their supply lines and communications. In the vastness of the desert, railways, roads, bridges and telegraph lines had become prime targets. Camel-mounted tribesmen, as well as Allied soldiers using cars and armoured cars, had shown how effective long-range raids could be. Apart from their immediate military impact, the Arab armies also caused huge confusion behind enemy lines. It is estimated that the campaign tied down somewhere between 20,000 to 30,000 Turkish troops in Arabia and this perhaps was its greatest achievement. It is difficult to arrive at final casualty figures for either side but it has been estimated that the Ottoman Army lost around 15,000 men, including those who succumbed to sickness.

The potential of using vehicles and planes had also been demonstrated and the Allied armies realized the importance of establishing desert supply depots to aid future operations. Combined with experience gained in Libya during the Senussi Revolt and the campaigns in Palestine, the basis for a new doctrine of desert warfare had been created. These methods would be returned to during World War II, especially by the SAS and the Long Range Desert Group during their campaign of raids in North Africa.

THE LAWRENCE LEGEND

Larger-than-life characters populated the history of the Arab Revolt. These included both Arabs and men of the Allied missions. In general, they have all receded into the background of history. In the decades that have followed an enormous amount of historical and public attention has been lavished on the history of the Arab Revolt. One figure has emerged and has remained pre-eminent in all the subsequent outpourings on the Arab Revolt of 1916–18: T. E. Lawrence.

In 1918, there was no indication that this would be the case. Lawrence was indeed one of the major figures of this campaign and had risen from being a lowly lieutenant to the rank of colonel in the space of just over two years. He had been made a CB and was also awarded a DSO, but he was just one of several distinguished Allied officers.

On his return to England in 1918, he remained passionately committed to the Arab cause and accompanied Feisal to the Paris Peace Conference of 1919. While at this conference, he began writing his memoir of the revolt. This would later be published as *Seven Pillars of Wisdom*. In June of 1919 he was elected as a research fellow of All Souls College in Oxford and it seemed that he might return to a scholarly life. 1919 can also be recognized as being a crucial year for Lawrence and also the beginning of the public acclaim that he later enjoyed.

A bronze bust of T. E. Lawrence by Eric Kennington. The original of this bust was placed in St Paul's Cathedral in London. Lawrence was sat for the original in 1926 when five casts were made, all of which are now in public collections. In the 1960s a further series of casts was made from the original plaster. This is the fourth casting from that series and it is in the collection of Trinity College, Dublin. (Reproduced by kind permission of the Board of Trinity College, Dublin)

During the war an American journalist, Lowell Thomas, had visited Arabia in 1918. He used the photographs that he had shot in Arabia as the basis for a series of public shows. The first of these appeared in London in August 1919. At a theatre in Covent Garden, Thomas opened a show entitled *With Allenby in Palestine*, which included a slideshow, a lecture and also music and dancing. He realized that it was Lawrence, the archaeologist turned soldier, who really grabbed the public's attention. A series of meetings between Thomas and Lawrence followed and Lawrence posed for further photographs. The new show was now entitled *With Allenby in Palestine and Lawrence in Arabia*. Its extended run in London was followed by a tour around England. By 1920, Lawrence was a household name.

Lawrence tried to use this popular interest to further his political aims as he increasingly spoke out against the settlements that were being imposed on the former Ottoman territories. In

1921 he was invited to join the Colonial Office as an adviser on Arab affairs and he took part in the Cairo Conference of the same year. It is now obvious that he became increasingly disillusioned with the post-war plans for Arabia. He could not convert his popular image into political pressure and he ultimately resigned from all offices and, it could be argued, turned his back on the world that he had known. In 1922, Lawrence could probably have chosen to follow a political, military or academic career, but instead chose to join the RAF as an enlisted man, assuming the name 'J. H. Ross'. Hounded from the RAF by press exposure, he enlisted in the Tank Corps in 1923, this time as 'T. E. Shaw'. He would later return to the RAF in 1925 and remain there, as an enlisted man, until his retirement in February 1935.

This enigmatic behaviour has fed public and scholarly interest ever since. Lawrence's biographers have included academics, former soldiers and also psychologists. Numerous reasons have been put forwards for the way he

Lt-Col. T.E. Lawrence, CB, DSO. James McBey painted this portrait in one sitting in Damascus in October 1918, just after the city fell to Arab and Allied forces. While Lawrence later sat for several other portraits there is a certain immediacy to McBey's portrait and it captures an exhausted Lawrence at the end of the desert campaign (see the photograph on page 76). McBey later recorded that several Arab chieftains came to bid farewell to Lawrence as he sat for this portrait. (Imperial War Museum, London. Art collection 2473)

removed himself from public life. These various motives have included theories of political disillusionment, difficulties with his sexuality, a crisis of identity and also the trauma of his wartime experiences. Perhaps all these factors played their part.

In the years that followed, he maintained a low profile within the RAF while at the same time he engaged in correspondence with a vast number of friends and acquaintances. These included literary figures, soldiers, politicians and academics. Lawrence also indulged in his love for speed. He had a series of high-powered Brough motorcycles and was involved in the development of high-speed RAF rescue boats.

Throughout his years in the RAF, Lawrence continued to develop the text of *Seven Pillars of Wisdom*. Having lost a draft at Reading Station in 1919, he rewrote the text and circulated proof copies of the new draft in 1922. In 1926 a subscribers' edition was issued and an abridgement of the text, entitled *Revolt in the Desert*, was published in 1927. This was well received by a public eager to read his memoirs. Further literary endeavours followed and Lawrence completed a new translation of Homer's *Odyssey* while also completing a memoir of his life in the ranks of the RAF in 1928. Entitled *The Mint*, this latter memoir would not be published until 1955, long after Lawrence's death, because of the frank nature of his revelations of life as a 'ranker'.

Lawrence's association with figures in the world of the arts resulted in his sitting for various portraits. Artists who painted him included James McBey, William Roberts and Augustus John. The artist Eric Kennington created a bust of Lawrence and this would later be used as a memorial in St Paul's Cathedral.

Having retired from the RAF in 1935, he went to live at his cottage at Clouds Hill in Dorset. Just a few months after his retirement, Lawrence was critically injured in a motorcycle accident. He died on 19 May 1935 and was buried at Moreton in Dorset. Among the mourners were Winston Churchill, General A. P. Wavell, Siegfried Sassoon and Augustus John. Eric Kennington would later create an effigy of Lawrence, in Arab robes, and this is in the church at St Martin's, Wareham, in Dorset.

The general publication of *Seven Pillars of Wisdom* in 1935 further fuelled the public interest in him. It remains one of the classics of 20th-century literature and is perhaps Lawrence's greatest and most long-lasting legacy. It has also fed much debate. It is typical of Lawrence that he was the only source for some of the most dramatic events of his life, such as the execution of Hamed the Moor in 1916 and the rape incident at Deraa in 1917. Generations of Lawrence scholars and enthusiasts have since debated the veracity of some of his claims. Also, in recent years, *Seven Pillars of Wisdom* has been returned to again by a new generation of military officers who are involved in the wars in Afghanistan and Iraq.

Lawrence has never receded totally from the public eye during the 20th century. His story spawned a whole literature and was also the focus of dramatic works. In 1960 Terence Rattigan's play *Ross* received wide acclaim in a London production, with Alec Guinness in the title role. It has since been produced in various theatres around the world. Alexander Korda had thought of producing a Lawrence movie in the 1930s but it was the 1962 movie *Lawrence of Arabia*, however, which presented Lawrence to a global audience once again. Directed by David Lean, the movie boasted a stellar cast including Anthony Quayle, Anthony Quinn, Jack Hawkins, Omar Sharif and Alec Guinness, but Lean chose to cast a virtual unknown, Peter O'Toole, as the enigmatic Lawrence. Regardless of its historical shortcomings and omissions,

it was a truly epic movie and is rightly seen as a classic. Lawrence has since been played by various actors including Ralph Fiennes in the TV drama *A dangerous man: Lawrence after Arabia* (1990).

The story of the Arab Revolt has remained inextricably entwined with that of Lawrence and it seems that he will remain in the central role in the literature and public perception of that episode. Lowell Thomas commented that Lawrence 'had a genius for backing into the limelight'. It was a perceptive comment and it remains true. Owing to his flamboyant yet enigmatic character, his literary style and his self-promotional abilities, T. E. Lawrence is perceived as *the* major figure of the Arab Revolt and has become one the iconic figures of the modern era. Lawrence once commented that 'Colonel Lawrence still goes on; only I have stepped out of the way.' Over 70 years after his death, this remains true.

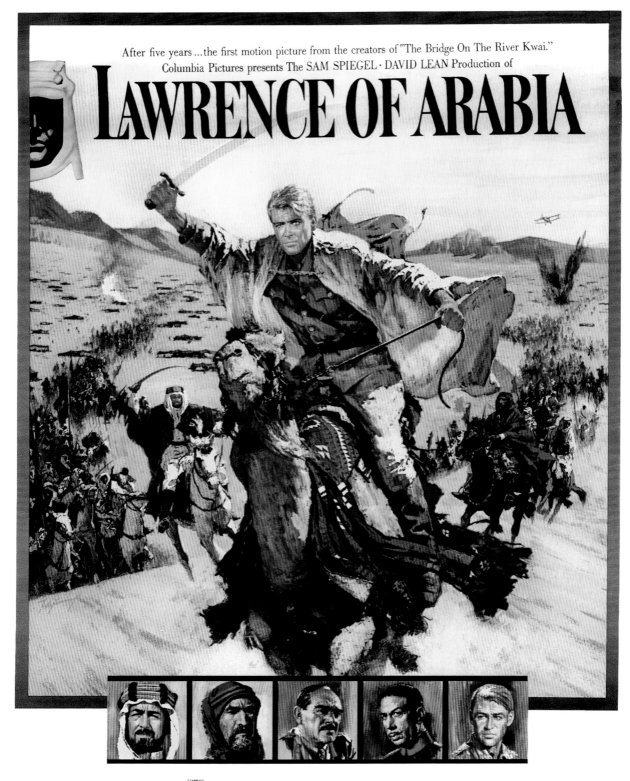

THE BATTLEFIELD TODAY

The Arab Revolt was a vast affair in geographical terms. To visit a cross section of the main sites of action of 1916–18 would mean touring modern-day Saudi Arabia, Jordan, Palestine, Lebanon and Syria. The port towns on the Red Sea that were so crucial to the revolt have all seen modern development. At the same time, the old town centres of Aqaba, Yanbu, Wejh and Jiddah retain some of their traditional character.

It is also still possible to trace the line of the old Hejaz Railway, and, while the line has fallen into disuse and been dismantled, traces do remain. Several of the old railway buildings survive in varying states of repair. The old station building at Ma'an in Jordan for example survives and it is intended that a new museum will be established there in the future. Conversely, the station at Batn Al Ghoul stands deserted and in disrepair. In some locations, locomotives that were wrecked during the Revolt remain marooned in the desert. The remains of a wrecked train lies in the desert south of Wayban while another lies in Hediyya Station in Saudi Arabia.

OPPOSITE PAGE
A movie poster for David Lean's 1962 film *Lawrence of Arabia*. This epic movie served to re-launch Lawrence to the wider world and still informs modern perceptions of Lawrence. (Author's collection)

RIGHT
An abandoned railway wagon of the defunct Hejaz Railway. It is still possible to find both locomotives and rolling stock that had been damaged in World War I. In this case, the wagon has been left to decay. (Courtesy of the Great Arab Revolt Project)

RIGHT
Members of the Great Arab
Revolt Project excavating a
Turkish command post at the
Hill of Birds, outside Ma'an, in
2006. This redoubt included
a series of boltholes in which
troops could take cover when
under shellfire. (Courtesy of
the Great Arab Revolt Project)

BELOW
A deserted station of the Hejaz
Railway at Wadi Rutm. It is
possible to trace the line of
the old railway and find the
scene of some of the raids of
1916–18. (Courtesy of the
Great Arab Revolt Project)

The town of Tafila, scene of the battle of January 1918 has grown bigger but the battlefield can still be found as can the small Ottoman fort in the town that stood in Lawrence's day. The castles at Kerak and Shawbak still stand, as does Lawrence's hideaway at Azrak (or Azraq) to the west of Amman. Several modern tour companies run special tours of areas associated with T. E. Lawrence. The vast canyon of Wadi Rum, so beloved of Lawrence, remains largely untouched. The nearby spring, known as 'Shallala' to the Bedu and described by Lawrence in *Seven Pillars of Wisdom*, can still be found.

In the last few years, the archaeology of the Arab Revolt has received new attention. The teams of the Great Arab Revolt Project have undertaken new excavations in Jordan, concentrating around Ma'an, and have uncovered much evidence of the Turkish entrenchments that once protected that area. It is hoped that this fieldwork will not only increase our knowledge of the Revolt but also encourage more tourism in the area. Each year, the GARP takes a number of paying volunteers and further information can be found on the project's website: http://www.jordan1914-18archaeology.org/

There are several places associated with Lawrence in England and through judicious reading of biographies, addresses where he lived in Oxford and London, can be identified. The Lawrence family home in Polstead Road is now a private residence. The City of Oxford High School for Boys that he attended can be easily found. Other Oxford locations associated with Lawrence include both Jesus College and All Souls College and the Ashmolean Museum. His last home at Clouds Hill in Dorset is a National Trust property.

A post-war photograph of an unidentified unit at Petra. The style of tunic and Sam Browne belt would suggest that these men are from the police or gendarmerie of Transjordan (modern-day Jordan). F. G. Peake or 'Peake Pasha', who had served in the Arab Revolt, organized a police force in Transjordan in 1921. The headgear of these two men suggests Circassian origins. (Courtesy of the Library of Congress)

FURTHER READING

Since the 1920s a huge literature on the Arab Revolt in general and T. E. Lawrence in particular has been created. Hardly a year passes without some new titles on the subject coming to print. It is impossible within the scope of this volume to provide an exhaustive list. The bibliography below can serve only as a guide for further reading. If one were to make one general point about the existing literature, it would be that the attention paid to T. E. Lawrence has created something of an imbalance and that this has meant that some of the other figures in the Arab Revolt have been largely overlooked.

Lawrence's own books on his career in Arabia are listed below. His epic memoir, *Seven Pillars of Wisdom*, was first published as a 'subscribers' only' edition in 1926 but was published for a wider audience in 1935. His *Revolt in the Desert* appeared in a public edition in 1927. Both have remained almost constantly in print ever since and can be found in various editions.

Asher, Michael, *Lawrence: the Uncrowned King of Arabia* Penguin, London, 1998

Barr, James, *Setting the Desert on Fire: T. E. Lawrence and Britain's Secret War in Arabia, 1916–18* Bloomsbury, London, 2006

Brown, Malcolm, *Lawrence of Arabia: the Life, the Legend* Thames & Hudson, London, 2005

Erickson, E., *Ordered to Die: a History of the Ottoman Army in World War One* Greenwood Press, London, 2001

Facey, William, and Najdat Fathi Safwat (eds), *A Soldier's Story from Ottoman Rule to Independent Iraq: the Memoirs of Jafar Pasha Al-Askari* 1st English edition, Arabian Publishing, London, 2003

Falls, Cyril, *Military Operations, Egypt and Palestine* 2 volumes, HMSO, London, 1930

Faulkner, Neil, 'View from the field: Jordan' in *Current World Archaeology*, No. 17, June–July 2006

Garnett, Edward (ed.), *The Letters of T. E. Lawrence* Doubleday, Doran & Company, London, 1938

Graves, Robert, *Lawrence and the Arabs* Jonathan Cape, London, 1927

Hughes, Matthew, *Allenby in Palestine: the Middle East Correspondence of Field-Marshal Viscount Allenby* Army Records Society, 2004

James, Lawrence, *The Golden Warrior: the Life and Legend of Lawrence of Arabia* Abacus, London, 1990

—— *Imperial Warrior: the Life and Times of Sir Edmund Allenby* Weidenfeld and Nicholson, London, 1993

Lawrence, T. E., *The Revolt in the Desert* 1st edition, Jonathan Cape, London, 1927

—— *Seven Pillars of Wisdom* Privately printed 1926, 1st public edition, Jonathan Cape, London, 1935

Leclerc, Christophe, *Avec T. E. Lawrence en Arabie: la mission militaire française au Hejaz, 1916–1920* Harmattan, Paris, 1998

Liddell Hart, Basil, *T. E. Lawrence in Arabia and after* Jonathan Cape, London, 1934

Mack, John E., *The Prince of our Disorder* Little, Brown & Company, London, 1978

Mousa, Suleiman, *T. E. Lawrence: an Arab View* Oxford University Press, Oxford, 1966

Nicolle, David, Men-at-Arms 208: *Lawrence and the Arab Revolts* Osprey Publishing Ltd, Oxford, 1989

—— Men-at-Arms 269: *The Ottoman Army, 1914–18* Osprey Publishing Ltd, Oxford, 1994

Nicholson, J., *The Hejaz Railway* Stacey International, London, 2005

Sanders, Liman von, *Five years in Turkey* Naval and Military Press, Annapolis, 1927

The Journal of the T. E. Lawrence Society

Wilson, Jeremy, *Lawrence of Arabia: the Authorised Biography* William Heinemann Ltd., London, 1989

INDEX

References to illustrations are shown in **bold**. Plates are shown with page locators in brackets.